Assemblies
A–Z

ASSEMBLIES
A–Z

C. M. Ward

BASIL BLACKWELL

First published 1984
Reprinted 1985

Published by
Basil Blackwell Limited
108 Cowley Road
Oxford OX4 1JF

British Library Cataloguing in Publication Data

Ward, C.M.
  Assemblies A – Z.
  1. Schools – Exercises and recreations
  I. Title
  377'.1   LB3015

ISBN 0 631 13468 9

Typeset in Palatino 11/12½ pt by
Freeman Graphic, Tonbridge, Kent
Printed in Great Britain

Contents

Preface

Assemblies A–Z comprises a collection of Christian–based assemblies for primary school worship. Quotations are from the *New English Bible* and the *Alternative Services Book*.

The suggested hymns for the assemblies have been selected from four publications:

Come and Praise (CP), BBC Publications;

One Hundred Hymns for Today (100 HT), William Clowes and Sons Limited;

Sing it in the Morning (SM), Thomas Nelson and Sons Limited;

With Cheerful Voice (WCV), Adam and Charles Black (Publishers) Limited.

Acknowledgements

The author and publisher would like to thank the following publishers for giving permission to reproduce material in this book:

P. Blakely, *Someone's Singing Lord*, Adam and Charles Black (Publishers) Limited: 179(3);

Prayers and collects from *The Alternative Service Book 1980* are © the Central Board of Finance of the Church of England and are reproduced with permission: 9(1), 18(2), 66(3), 74(1), 94(3), 103(1), 121(4), 140(1), 143(1), 153(1), 159(1), 193(1,2), 194(1,2), 195(5), 196(1); reproduced by kind permission of the Central Board of Finance of the Church of England, *In Excelsis*, CIO Publishing: 3(3);

M.E. Rose, *Morning Cockerel*, Granada Publishing Limited: 5(1,2), 29(3), 39(1), 102(2), 190(3), 195(3);

D. Baker, *Thy Kingdom Come*, Society for Promoting Christian Knowledge: 8(3);

M. Kitson, *Infant Prayer*: 113(3); *The Daily Service*, Oxford University Press: 119(1) (author G.W. Briggs);

A.G. Patston, *Assemblies for Primaries*, Religious and Moral Education Press: 141(1) (author A.G. Patston).

Every effort has been made to trace the source of copyright material and it is regretted if any acknowledgement has been unwittingly omitted.

A is for Action

The Good Samaritan

Action is a very good word to start a new year with. Action means doing things, not just sitting back and hoping everything will turn out the way we want it. We have to be the 'doers', the ones who will bring about the changes we want to see. One of the books in the New Testament is called the Acts of the Apostles, and it tells how the first friends of Jesus started to carry out his work for him, to go to all the different parts of the world to tell the people about Jesus and to baptise them and teach them.

Jesus was once talking to a lawyer who wanted to know what he must do to become a Christian. Jesus told him to love God with all his heart, his soul and his strength and to love his neighbour as much as he loved himself. The lawyer then wanted to know who his neighbour was, so Jesus told him the story of the Good Samaritan (Luke 10: 25–37). It tells of a man who set out on a journey from Jerusalem to Jericho, but on the way he was robbed and wounded and left to die by the side of the road. Neither the priest nor the Levite would stop to help, for they were afraid that the robbers might still be somewhere near, but the Samaritan did all that he could for the poor man, without thinking about himself. He put bandages on the man's wounds and took him to an inn and stayed with him for a time. When he had to leave, he left money with the innkeeper to take care of the poor traveller until he was well enough to set off again.

At the end of the story, the lawyer clearly understood who is heighbour should be. Jesus said to him, "Go and do as he did." This then means action. We, too, must set out in the year ahead to go and do what the Samaritan in the story did, and be friendly and cheerful and help whoever we can.

~ ~ ~ ~ ~ ~ ~ ~ ~ ~ ~ ~ ~

A is for Action (2)

Elizabeth Fry

There are lots of people who have done things to make people's lives better. Can you think of any? They have not all been important people, but they have all been people who really wanted to help *everyone*. They wanted to make life fair and just to all people. These people have been 'doers' and not just 'moaners'. So they became famous and we can read about them.

One person like this was Elizabeth Fry. She lived about a hundred and fifty years ago, at a time when there were lots of very poor people indeed, and not very much help for poor sick people, and where life in prisons was especially dreadful. Elizabeth was one of a large family. The family belonged to the Society of Friends, called the Quakers, who are especially concerned in making people's daily lives better. Elizabeth learned to think deeply about all these things. She felt that she had to do something in her life but for a long time she was not sure what.

When she married, Elizabeth came to London. She was very unhappy about all the dreadful things she saw in the great city. When she visited Newgate prison, she saw for herself the awful conditions the prisoners were expected to live in. People felt sorry for them, but little had been done to make things better. Elizabeth felt she had to help.

Elizabeth was married and she had eleven children of her own. She was so good at looking after people that she was always being asked to help out. But Elizabeth was never too busy to help when people asked for her. She was rather a shy person and she never wanted the lime-light or to put herself forward. She quietly did the best she could around the house and among her family.

One day, a man called Grollet, asked Elizabeth to visit Newgate prison. The prison officers didn't want to let her in, because the women prisoners were so wild and savage. But Elizabeth insisted. She came back many times to help the people inside the prison. She formed a little band of women, who collected clothing for the prisoners and their children. She organised a school for the children. She listened to the troubles of the women. She helped to clean up some of the worst of the mess and always, before she came away, she said a few words that she thought might help. Elizabeth asked the government to give the prisoners some useful work to do, which in the end they did.

Another terrible thing that used to happen to some of

the prisoners was that they were deported. They were sent far away from England, often to little known countries like Australia, where they had to fend for themselves. When Elizabeth found out how miserable those poor people were, she made sure that she visited every ship that was carrying convicts before it set sail. She tried to calm the prisoners down. Little by little people heard about all Elizabeth Fry's good work. Gradually the government made life in prisons less terrible. All the things she did made her life famous. She will be honoured for all time. But Elizabeth, did not look for glory herself. She had a true Christian spirit and she always prayed for guidance as she went about her work.

Prayers

1   Lord Jesus, show us something to do for you, something loving to say, something kind to do, somebody to comfort, something lovely to make. Help us to watch with your eyes for chances to do your work, because we love you. Amen.

2   Jesus, friend of the friendless, helper of the poor, healer of the sick, whose life was spent in doing good, let us follow in your footsteps. Make us strong to do right, gentle with the weak, and kind to all who are in sorrow, that we may be like you, our Lord and Master. Amen.

3   May our mouths praise the love of God this morning,
      O God may we do your will this day. May our ears
        hear the words of God and obey them,
      O God may we do your will this day. May our feet
        follow the footsteps of God in all that we do,
      O God, may we do your will this day. Amen.

Hymns

The wise may bring their learning (WCV 48)
There was a man on a long long journey-o (SM 23)

~ ~ ~ ~ ~ ~ ~ ~ ~ ~ ~ ~

A is for Advent

Preparing for Christmas

Advent Sunday, at the end of November, is the beginning of the year in the Christian Church. Advent is a time of preparation for Christmas, when we think about the birth of Jesus. The weeks before Christmas are always very busy for everybody. There is so much to do: shopping, cooking, packing parcels, making decorations, parties to plan and all the exciting things which might make us forget what it is that we are really celebrating. During Advent we remember the baby whose birthday we celebrate at Christmas. God gave us the greatest gift, his only son, that first Christmas Day. People had waited years and years for the Messiah, the king who was to be the Prince of Peace. The word Advent means 'coming'. It is taken from a Latin word. Latin is a language which is no longer spoken.

Jesus was born and when he grew up he taught his people. He wanted people to love each other, care for each other and be forgiving. He wanted them to open their hearts and make room for him in their lives. He said to them "Be awake, for you do not know on what day the Lord is to come. He may come at a time when you least expect him." (Matthew 24: 42)

The parable of the ten bridesmaids

Jesus told a parable about ten girls who were chosen to be bridesmaids to explain what he meant. (Matthew 25: 1–13). The wedding was late at night and the bridesmaids had to be ready to go out and meet the bridegroom. Each bridesmaid had a lantern. Five of them took extra oil with them so that their lamps keep burning brightly. The other five were foolish and carried no spare oil. The bridesmaids had a long time to wait, and they all fell asleep. At about midnight there was great excitement and they heard people calling out "Here is the bridegroom. Come and meet him." Then the five foolish girls asked the others to give them some oil, because their lamps would not burn. But the others had none left over. The five thoughtful girls hurried out to meet the groom. The other five hurried to buy more oil but when they got back the wedding procession had already gone and they were left behind. When they arrived at the wedding the door had been locked and although they knocked and begged to be let in, the voice from inside said, "I declare, I do not know you." So the story finishes with a warning, "Keep awake then, for you never know the day or the hour."

Let us then think about all that Advent means to us.

Prayers

1   O Lord, who loves all mankind, may your kingdom come within our hearts, within our homes, through all our land and throughout the world. Amen.

2   Help us, O Lord, always to wait for you, to wish for you and to watch for you, that at your coming again you may find us ready. Amen.

3   O Heavenly Father, we thank you for your gift to the world of your son, Jesus Christ our Lord. As we think of the coming of Jesus, help us to make ready a place in our hearts for him and to look for him day by day. Amen.

Hymns

Hills of the north rejoice (WCV 69)
When the herds were watching (WCV 90)

~ ~ ~ ~ ~ ~ ~ ~ ~ ~ ~ ~

A is for Allah

Muhammad and the Muslim faith

The Muslim word for God is Allah. When a baby is born into a Muslim family, a special word is whispered into each of the baby's ears. The words tell the baby to worship Allah and to love Muhammad, Allah's prophet.

Muhammad lived many hundreds of years ago in the country we now call Saudi Arabia. Before he was six years old both his father and his mother died, and Muhammad became an orphan. But he had a very kind uncle who looked after him like his own son. Muhammed became a shepherd and he spent many hours on the hillside, watching his sheep, but sometimes he travelled with camel trains through Arabia.

When Muhammad was by himself he liked to recite poems about Allah. He felt very close to his God when he was in the mountains, and sometimes he was sure there were angels near. One day the angel Gabriel spoke to Muhammad. The angel spoke through Muhammad to teach the people more about Allah's holy ways. These words of Muhammad were later written down, and they became the scriptures or laws of Islam. The *Koran*, as this special book is called, is like the Bible to the people of Muslim faith.

Muhammad had many children, but all except one died before him. His wife believed all that Muhammad was told by Allah and she encouraged him to share his wisdom. The people followed him as a prophet and Muhammad became a leader of his people. He taught them that everything that happens is the will of Allah and that they should not question his ways. Muhammad lived at a time when there was a lot of fighting among the people and he helped to unite them. Those who did not worship Allah were allowed to practise their own beliefs, and Muhammad did much to help the suffering of the poor.

Before he died, Muhammad made a pilgrimage to the sacred city of Mecca and to this day all Muslims try to visit Mecca once in their lifetime. When Muslims pray, they kneel and face Mecca and bow their heads onto the ground and call upon Allah to hear them. They remember Muhammad and worship him as one of Allah's holy prophets.

Prayers

1   O God our Father, we thank you for the freedom which is ours to worship you in the way that we choose. We thank you for the leaders of men who have helped to win this privilege for us. Amen.

2   Lord God, grant us to love you, grant that we may love those that love you, grant that we may do the deeds that win your love, make our love of you dearer to us than ourselves, our families and our wealth. Amen.

3   Give glory to God when you enter the darkness of night and when you enter the light of the morning, unto him be praise in the skies and on earth. Amen.

Hymns

New every morning is the love (WCV 2)
In Christ there is no East or West (WCV 47)

~ ~ ~ ~ ~ ~ ~ ~ ~ ~ ~ ~

A is for Altar

The Last Supper and Holy Communion

When we go into a Church we see many unfamiliar things. The seats are different from our chairs at school. Some of the windows have beautiful coloured glass which is made into pictures. But there is something which looks familiar and that is the table we all look at in Church. On it stands a cross, and at either side are candles which are lit for special services and festivals. This table is the altar. At the altar the priest blesses the bread and the wine for the service of Holy Communion.

Jesus told his friends that when he went back to his father in Heaven, they should remember him by sharing together the bread and the wine, his body and his blood. Before Jesus left, he went with his friends to Jerusalem to celebrate the feast of the Passover. On the day which we now call Palm Sunday he entered Jerusalem, riding on a donkey. The people cheered him and welcomed him as their long awaited king. But Jesus had enemies too, in Jerusalem. They were jealous of Jesus and of the influence he had on his disciples. His enemies felt that the teaching of Jesus was dangerous, for it meant they would lose some of their power. Whilst Jesus was in Jerusalem, they were plotting his death. Jesus knew what was going on in the minds of these men. he could have made his escape and taken an easy way out, but he knew what God had planned for him. He knew that the time would soon come when he would die on the Cross and he wanted his friends, his chosen disciples, to understand all that was going to happen.

Jesus sent Peter and John to prepare the passover supper for him to share with his disciples. (Luke 21: 7–20) Peter and John did as Jesus asked and made ready the room upstairs in the house that Jesus had chosen. When they were all gathered round the table Jesus took a cup of wine and after giving thanks he said, "Take this and share

7

it among yourselves." And he took bread, gave thanks and broke it, and he gave it to them with the words: "This is my body."

When we are in church and we look towards the altar it reminds us of Jesus and his death on the cross. We kneel at the altar to receive the blessing from the priest and, as soon as we are old enough, to share in the taking of the bread and the wine. From the altar, the priest gives us God's blessing before we leave the church and go out into the world to put Jesus's words into action as we try to follow his example.

Prayers

1　Dear Jesus, we thank you for our Church where we can worship you. Help us, as we kneel at the altar, to think about you, to be brave, as you were brave, and to follow your example. Amen.

2　Thank you Jesus for feeding us with the bread and wine, symbols of your body and your blood. Make us try our best to serve you with all our hearts, our minds and our strength. Amen.

3　Jesus who died for me
　　Help me to live for Thee. Amen.

Hymns

Praise my soul the King of Heaven (WCV 18)
In Christ there is no East or West (WCV 47)

~ ~ ~ ~ ~ ~ ~ ~ ~ ~ ~ ~

A is for Andrew

Fishers of men

St Andrew's Day is on the last day of November. St Andrew is the patron saint of Scotland and so it is an important date for the people of Scotland. The cross of St Andrew makes up part of the flag of Great Britain, which is called the Union Jack. The name Andrew comes from Greek, and it means a strong man. Andrew, one of the first disciples of Jesus, was certainly a strong man. He was a brave man who served Jesus all his life and he died on a cross because he refused to betray his faith. Today there are many churches names after St Andrew, and Andrew is still a popular name for parents to choose for their sons. Anyone who has the name Andrew has a name he should feel very proud of. He has a fine example to follow if he tries to be like Andrew.

When Jesus called Andrew to work for him he said "Come, follow me, and I will make you fishers of men." (Matthew 4:19) Andrew left his work as a fisherman and gladly went with Jesus. From his disciples Jesus chose the twelve apostles, and Andrew and his brother Simon Peter were both among them. Andrew must have felt very proud when Jesus announced the names of the twelve chosen to be the Apostles. (Luke 6: 12–16)

Feeding of the five thousand

In the gospels we read of the wonderful miracle of Jesus' feeding of five thousand people. The gospel of St John tells us that Andrew was one of the disciples with Jesus that day. (John 6: 1–14) It had been a busy day beside the sea of Galilee where Jesus had been teaching the people and healing the sick. He went up the hillside to sit down with his disciples, but great crowds of people began to gather. Jesus was anxious and concerned for them. He wanted to give them food to eat because they had walked a long way to find him and still had a long journey back. He asked his disciples where they could buy food. Philip replied that they hadn't enough money to buy bread for so many people. Then Andrew found a boy who had with him five barley loaves and two small fishes, but he said "What is that among so many?" But Jesus knew what he was going to do. When all the people were sitting down on the grass, Jesus took first the loaves and then the fishes and blessed them. All the five thousand people on the hillside were fed and they all had enough to eat. When everyone had finished, Jesus told the disciples to gather up all that was left over, so that nothing should be wasted and they filled twelve baskets with the remains. When the people saw what Jesus had done, they said, "Surely this must be the prophet that was to come into the world."

Prayers

1   Almighty God, who gave such grace to your apostle, St Andrew, that he readily obeyed the call of your son

and brought his brother with him, give us, who are called by your holy word, grace to follow without delay and to tell the good news of your kingdom; through Jesus Christ our Lord. Amen.

2   O Lord Jesus help us to be strong, as Andrew was strong, and to love and serve you all our lives. Amen.

3   Lord, on the way to goodness, when we stumble, hold us; when we fall, lift us up; when we are hard pressed by evil, deliver us; when we turn from what is good, turn us back, and bring us at last to your glory. Amen.

Hymns

Fill thou my life, O Lord my God (CP 41)
Spirit of God as strong as the wind (CP 63)

~ ~ ~ ~ ~ ~ ~ ~ ~ ~ ~ ~

B is for Baptism
The baptism of Christ

Jesus was baptised when he was a man and was just beginning the special work which God had sent him into the world to do. Jesus went to the River Jordan to find his cousin John. John had been preaching about the coming of Jesus and telling people to be sorry for their sins and to try to lead better lives. He was surprised and pleased to see Jesus, but when Jesus told John that he wanted him to baptise him, John replied that he was not good enough. (Matthew 3: 13–17) But Jesus told John that it was God's wish and so they both went into the river and Jesus was baptised. When he came out of the water he saw the spirit of God coming down from heaven and a voice said, "This is my son, my beloved, on whom my favour rests."

Before he died on the Cross, Jesus told his special friends to teach men all over the world and to baptise them in the name of the Father, the Son and the Holy Spirit. (Matthew 28: 19) Peter, as soon as he had received the Holy Spirit, started to teach. On that first day about three thousand people who heard his words were baptised. (Acts 2: 41)

Infant baptism

When you are baptised you promise to turn to Christ and give up evil. You declare your belief in God the Father, God the Son and God the Holy Spirit, and your faith in the Church. Small babies cannot make these promises for themselves so each child is given godparents who make the promises for them. The godparents also promise to see that their godchildren grow up to learn about Jesus and his teaching, and encourage them to go to church to make these promises for themselves when they are old enough. When we are baptised we are given our first names, our Christian names, and we become part of God's family. I expect you all know how many Christian names you have but you might like to go home and ask who your godparents are. They are probably among your aunts and uncles. Your parents can also tell you which church you were christened in and who took the service. The vicar writes the names of all the people he has christened in a big register which he keeps in the church.

11

The Christening Service takes place at the font and during the service the vicar pours a little water onto the baby's forehead and marks it with the sign of the cross. When he does this he says, "I sign you with the cross, the sign of Christ. Do not be ashamed to confess the faith of Christ crucified." (ASB p245) And so, when we are baptised, we become one in the great number of disciples who promise to love and serve the Lord Jesus.

Prayers

1   We thank you, God, for our baptism to life in Christ and we pray for all children. Heavenly Father, in your love you have called us to know you, led us to trust you and bound our life with yours. Surround us with your love, protect us from evil and fill us with your Holy Spirit. Walk with us in the way of Christ and help us to grow in the knowledge of your love. Amen.

2   Help us, O God, to fight valiantly under the banner of Christ against sin, the word and the devil. Make us faithful soldiers and servants to the end of our lives. Amen.

3   Day by day, dear Lord of Thee three things I pray,
    To see thee more clearly, Love Thee more dearly,
    Follow Thee more nearly
    Day by day. Amen.

Hymns

O Jesus I have promised (WCV 41)
We are climbing Jesus' ladder (CP 49)

~ ~ ~ ~ ~ ~ ~ ~ ~ ~ ~ ~

B is for Bartimaeus

The blind

This morning we are going to think about people who are blind. Sight is a wonderful gift which we may often take for granted. Everything that we do – work, play, recognising our family, friends, people and objects around us – depends on sight. We can see the colour in the world around and notice tiny details and patterns. We can tell one flower from another, one tree from another or even one jumper or pair of socks from another. What a lot we have to be thankful for.

We can show our gratitude by the care we give to people who are blind. These people are very brave and they do not give up because they cannot see where they are going or what they are doing. They learn to listen carefully and to recognise people by their voices and footsteps. Blind people are taught to read with their fingers using special books. These books are written in Braille and have raised dots instead of letters written in ink. Blind people sometimes use a white stick to show that they cannot see, and all of you must have seen the guide dogs for the blind carefully leading their owners in the busy streets. Modern medicine has helped a lot and so these days there are probably fewer people who suffer from blindness than in the days of Jesus. We know that Jesus felt very concerned whenever the sick, the deaf, the lame or the blind were brought to him. We can read about the wonderful miracles he performed as he gave back sight to the blind.

Jesus' healing of Bartimaeus

One day Jesus and his disciples came to Jericho. Crowds of people had gathered to see Jesus and Bartimaeus, a blind beggar, was among them. Of course, he could not see what was going on, but he was listening to everything. He must have had great hope because when he heard that Jesus of Nazareth was coming to the town, he shouted, "Jesus, Son of David, have pity on me." Many people tried to make Bartimaeus stop shouting, but Bartimaeus only called out even more loudly, "Son of David, have pity on me." As Jesus got nearer and heard Bartimaeus shouting at the top of his voice, he stopped. Jesus looked around the crowd and said "Call him", so they went to Bartimaeus and said, "Jesus is waiting for you, Come." Bartimaeus did not waste a minute. He jumped to his feet straight away and was brought to Jesus. Jesus said to him, "What do you want me to do for you?" Bartimaeus answered quite simply, "Master, I want my sight back." And then Jesus spoke these wonderful words, "Go, your faith has cured you." Bartimaeus found that his sight was restored immediately. He was full of joy and he followed Jesus on his way.

Let us try to use our eyes to see whom we can help and then to find a way to be of service.

Prayers

1 O God who has given us eyes to see
The colours, that are here and there.
Give us a heart to find out thee
And see your presence everywhere. Amen.

2 Loving Father, we are sorry for people who are blind and cannot see the blue sky, the sunshine, the green fields, the trees and the flowers, and who cannot see to read, write, work or play. We ask you to bless and comfort them. Please help us always to be kind to blind people and to try to make them happy. Amen.

3 O Lord God we thank you for the most precious gift of sight. With our eyes we can behold the beauty and wonder of your great creation. With our hearts we thank you for the richness of our lives. Amen.

Hymns

There is singing in the desert (CP 25)
Lord, we are blind (100 HT 66)

~ ~ ~ ~ ~ ~ ~ ~ ~ ~ ~ ~

B is for Bethlehem
The birth of Jesus
O little town of Bethlehem
How still we see Thee lie.

These are the opening words of a popular carol we sing at Christmas time. Bethlehem was the town where Mary and Joseph had to go to pay their taxes on the orders of Emperor Augustus, and it was there that Jesus was born. The birth of Jesus made Bethlehem a famous place. Many people still travel to the Holy Land to see the stable where Jesus was born, the places where he grew up and the towns he travelled to.

Before Jesus was born Bethlehem was not an important place. It was a quiet village surrounded by hills where the shepherds watched their sheep. The women would go to the well for their water, the men would sell their wares in

14

the market place just as they did in all the other little towns round about. Life was very quiet. There were no cars, trains or aeroplanes, radio or television, holidays abroad and not many visitors. The crowds of people who came to Bethlehem to be registered at the City of David the year that Jesus was born must have caused a lot of interest for the local people. All the inns were full and when Mary and Joseph arrived there was no room left.

Years and years before, the prophet Micah had said that from Bethlehem would come a governor for Israel. (Micah 5: 2) King Herod's advisers remembered the words of the prophet when the wise men went to his court in Jerusalem to ask where they could find the newborn king. King Herod was very surprised at the question, but his priests and lawyers said that the baby would be born at Bethlehem in Judaea because they remembered the prophecy. "Bethlehem in the land of Judah, you are far from least in the eyes of the ruler of Judah, for out of you shall come a leader to be the shepherd of my people, Israel." (Matthew 2: 2–6)

Ruth and Naomi

In the lovely story of Ruth and Naomi in the Old Testament, we are told that Naomi wanted to go back to her home town of Bethlehem after her husband had died. Ruth did not want Naomi to have to make a new life on her own and so she too went to Bethlehem to be with her. When they got to Bethlehem it was harvest time and Ruth went to gather what food she could, so that she and Naomi would be able to live through the winter months. Ruth and Naomi both settled happily into their new life at Bethlehem.

Perhaps one day, you too, will visit Bethlehem and then you will see the fields where Ruth went to work, the hillside where the shepherds heard the message of the angels and you may walk along the same streets travelled by Mary and Joseph themselves.

Prayers

1 Dear loving Father, as we remember the journey of Mary and Joseph to Bethlehem, help us to think of our mothers and fathers and to thank you for giving us

homes of our own and families to which we belong. We thank you for your own home town and we ask that we may grow up to be useful and caring citizens. Amen.

2   Thank you God for the places we know and the places we visit. Be with those who have to travel to strange places and who have to make their homes in towns where they are strangers. Amen.

3   Jesus, we know how much you love us, and that you are with us always and in all places. Be with us wherever we go and help us to remember that you are always near us and that your love surrounds us. Amen.

Hymns

O little town of Bethlehem (WCV 97)
Come and praise the Lord our King (CP 21)

~ ~ ~ ~ ~ ~ ~ ~ ~ ~ ~ ~ ~

B is for Bible

Mary Jones

From the Bible we can learn of the lives of famous men and women who lived long before Jesus was born. The Old Testament tells us about the men of faith who trusted in God and about the promise which God made to his people that one day he would send to them the Messiah. We can read how God made the word and everything in it and we can learn how all through the years men worshipped God in their different ways.

In the New Testament we can read about the life and teachings of Jesus, how Christianity began and how the apostles went out to tell the good news of Christ's kingdom. All this information we have in one book, the Bible, but the Bible itself is made up of many books, written by different people. There are sixty-five books altogether: thirty-nine in the Old Testament and twenty-six in the New Testament. The Bible has been translated into many languages, so that people in all parts of the world can read and understand its message.

A young Welsh girl once badly wanted a Bible of her own. Her name was Mary Jones and she lived with her father and mother in a quiet little village. Mary's parents were not rich but they loved their daughter, and Mary grew up very happily. Every week the family went to church and there Mary heard the stories from the Bible. She thought how wonderful it would be if she could have a Bible of her very own. But Bibles were very expensive and Mary could not read. Still, she had set her heart on having a Bible. When Mary started school, a kind neighbour promised her that if she learnt to read, then she could visit her house and read from her Bible. So Mary worked hard so that she could read this wonderful book for herself. How proud she felt when she first managed to read some of the verses on her own. Now more than ever she wanted her own Bible so that she could read whenever she wished.

So Mary began to work. She did as many errands and jobs as she could to earn the money that she needed to buy the precious book. It took a long time but eventually Mary saved enough. The nearest shop where she could buy a Bible was twenty-five miles away. Mary would have to walk all the way, but she set out and eventually found the shop. There were three copies of the Bible left and each one had been promised to somebody else. Mary was so bitterly disappointed she could not hide her tears. The kindly shopkeeper was so sorry for her that he gave her his own Bible. It made him realise how great was the need of the poorer people as well as of the rich to own a Bible and so he formed a society to make Bibles readily available to everyone. Now the Bible reaches people all over the world and is written in more than a thousand languages.

Prayers

1   We thank you, Heavenly Father, for the Bible which is your word to us. We thank you for the wonderful stories of Jesus, our friend and saviour. Help us to read, and learn and understand, so that we may be like him. Amen.

2   Blessed Lord, who caused all holy scriptures to be written for our learning, help us to hear them, to read, mark, learn and inwardly digest them that, through patience, and the comfort of your holy word, we may embrace and for ever hold fast the hope of everlasting

life, which you have given us in our Saviour, Jesus Christ. Amen.

3   Thank you, Lord, for those who gave their lives to give us the Bible in our own language. Please help those who are translating and printing the Bible in faraway places, so that one day the Bible may be read in all the languages of the world. Bless those who teach us to understand what the Bible means, in our own country as well as in other lands. Amen.

Hymns

Praise we now the word of grace (100 HT 84)
Heavenly Father may thy blessing (CP 62)

~ ~ ~ ~ ~ ~ ~ ~ ~ ~ ~ ~

C is for Centurion

The healing of the centurion's servant

The land where Jesus lived was ruled by the Romans. Soldiers were always on the streets of the towns and cities, and the people who lived there often hated them. The people did not like having to pay taxes to the Romans and they did not like having to obey foreigners who told them what they must do. A lot of people believed that when their own king came, as God had promised, he would change their lives. When Jesus came he was a man of peace. He told the people that they should obey those who rules over them and that they should be friendly towards the strangers in their land. Jesus said they should pay Caesar what was due to Caesar, and pay God what was due to God. (Matthew 22: 21)

The captains in the army of the Romans were called centurions. In the Bible we can read of one very good centurion. (Matthew 8: 5–10) This man came to Jesus one day because his servant was ill. He was afraid the servant might die and he wanted to help him. He had already done all he could, but his young servant was growing weaker all the time. So the centurion went and found Jesus and said to him, "Sir, a boy of mine lies at home paralysed and in great pain." Jesus answered at once that he would go home with the centurion and cure his servant. He was surprised when the Roman soldier said, "Why should you come to my house? There is no need. You have only to speak the word and my servant will be healed." The centurion then told Jesus that he was used to giving orders and being obeyed. If he said to his soldiers "Go", they went, and if he ordered them to come, they came at once. When he told them to do something, it was done instantly. If he, a centurion, could command such authority, he knew that Jesus had only to say his servant should be healed, and this would happen.

Jesus was amazed when he heard the Roman soldier declare his faith in him. He was very moved and he said to the people following him that he had never before come across anyone who trusted in him so completely. Jesus then turned to the centurion and said to him, "Go home now. Because of your faith, so let it be." And the Bible tells us that at that moment the boy recovered.

19

This was a wonderful miracle because it also shows us how great Jesus' power to help us is if we put all our trust and faith in him.

Prayers

1 O Lord, whose way is perfect, help us always to trust in your goodness, that walking with you and following you, we may always have quiet and contented minds, for you care for us all. Amen.

2 Lord Jesus, we ask that we may have such faith in you that we may turn to you always in times of difficulty, knowing that you are there to guide us and protect us. Amen.

3 O Loving Father of us all,
Who by your power has set us free,
O may we answer to your call,
And evermore to trust in three.
There's nothing more we need to ask,
But faith to follow you until,
We've overcome and done the task
That's set, because it is your will. Amen.

Hymns

Not far beyond the sea (100 HT 68)
There's a child in the streets (CP 27)

~ ~ ~ ~ ~ ~ ~ ~ ~ ~ ~ ~ ~

C is for Children

Blessed by Jesus

When Jesus began his teaching he often talked about children. He once told the people he was speaking to that they must all become like children if they wanted to enter the Kingdom of Heaven. Jesus also told his disciples that anyone who gave even a cup of cold water to one of his little ones would not go unrewarded. (Matthew 10: 42)

The story we all know best about Jesus and children is about the day when he blessed a number of children. It was late in the day and Jesus had stopped for a little while to rest. The disciples knew he must be tired because he usually welcomed the people who gathered to listen to him, or to try to touch him. His friends wanted him to enjoy a little peace, and so when they saw that groups of children were coming closer and closer to Jesus they tried to turn them away. Jesus noticed what his disciples were doing and he spoke to them sternly. He said they were to bring the children to him and certainly not to send them away, and then Jesus blessed each child.

Prayers

1   Jesus, friend of little children,
    Be a friend to me,
    Take my hand and ever keep me
    Close to thee. Amen.

2   Dear Lord Jesus, we are thankful for our true friends, but we would have you for our dearest friend. Let us love all our friends, but love you most of all. Make us, like you, a friend to all children. Amen.

3   It fell upon a summer's day,
    When Jesus walked in Galilee,
    The mothers from a village brought
    Their children to his knee.
    He took them in his arms, and laid
    His hands on each remembered head.
    "Suffer these little ones to come
    To me," he gently said. Amen.

4   Jesus, friend of children, be my friend.
    Teach me your courage and endurance,
    Your kindness to all in sickness or sorrow:
    Let my hands work for you,
    My feet be swift to run your errands of mercy:
    And make me proud to be your friend.

Hymns

It fell upon a summer's day (WCV 63)
Can you count the stars (WCV 77)

~ ~ ~ ~ ~ ~ ~ ~ ~ ~ ~ ~

C is for Commandments

The ten commandments

Long before Jesus was born, God gave Moses ten laws or commandments so that Moses could explain them to the people. He had helped the people of Israel escape from the land of Egypt and now he wanted them to be faithful to God who had guided them to freedom. Moses went up to the top of Mount Sinai and God promised him that if he and his people followed his commandments, then the Israelites would be his chosen people. When Moses climbed Mount Sinai the people were told to wait at the bottom. There was a great storm of thunder and lightning and the whole mountain seemed to shake. Moses told the people not to be afraid. God was putting them to the test and Moses went to meet God through a dark cloud. (Exodus 20: 21)

The ten laws that God gave Moses were written down on stone tablets and these commandments are still read out in the Communion Service in Church. Jesus gave a new commandment: love one another.

Commandments are rules or laws that every one should obey. Very often rules are about safety. We all know that we have to obey the Green Cross Code when we want to cross the road. If we did not stop, look and listen we would get run over. We know that we must not eat berries that grow on hedges because some may be poisonous. We must not touch medicine bottles even though some coloured pills look like sweets.

Our rules at school are to keep everybody safe and happy. We say that you must not run round corners or fight in the playground or carry umbrellas which might poke other people's eyes, or wear rings which might accidentally scratch another child. We ask you to tie back your long hair so that you can see better when you work, and always to use your hankie when you sneeze, so that you do not spread germs to other people. Every rule, law or commandment has a reason, and should be obeyed.

Let us pray that our hearts may be filled with love so that we may try and obey all God's holy laws and commandments.

Prayers

1 Almighty and most merciful Father, who has given us a new commandment that we should love one another, give us also grace that we may fulfil it. Make us gentle, courteous, obedient and forgiving, for the sake of Jesus Christ our Lord. Amen.

2 Bless, O Lord Jesus, our parents and all who love us and take care of us. Make us loving towards them and helpful and kind in all that we do. Amen.

3 Help us, O Lord, to put you first, others next and ourselves last, now and always. Amen.

Hymns

O worship the King all glorious above (WCV 14)
Heavenly Father may thy blessing (WCV 16)

~ ~ ~ ~ ~ ~ ~ ~ ~ ~ ~ ~ ~

D is for Daniel
Daniel and the lions' den

Daniel was a Jewish boy. He was taken when he was young to the city of Babylon where he was trained to serve the king in his palace. Many other young boys were also taken prisoner, and Daniel had three special friends among them. All the boys worked hard, and when they were older and well-trained they were presented to King Nebuchadnezzar at his court. The king was very pleased with the boys, especially with Daniel, and gradually he gave them positions of responsibility and power.

But all the time he was at the king's court, Daniel never forgot the true God whose commands he always tried to obey. Daniel would not touch the meat and rich wines which were offered to him. He ate vegetables and drank water instead. He prayed to God every day, throwing open his window and kneeling towards Jerusalem, the royal city of the Jews.

Daniel was a fair and kind person and every one respected him. He pleased the king by telling him what his dreams meant, and the king trusted in Daniel. When the old king died, Daniel served his son, King Belshazzar, and later he served King Darius. However, because the king liked him so much, some of the other princes and leaders grew jealous of Daniel. They tried to find faults in him so that they could report them to the king. But Daniel's behaviour was always honourable. The wicked men then began to plot against Daniel. They knew King Darius was a proud man and so they went to him and suggested that he should make a new law. This law said that for thirty days, no one should pray to any god or ask help from anyone except King Darius himself. Darius was pleased with the idea and so he passed the new law. Then those who had plotted against Daniel watched to see what he would do. Daniel knew that the punishment for anyone who broke this law was to be thrown into a den of lions!

But Daniel was a brave man. Whatever happened, he knew that he must do what was right, and so he continued to pray to the God he worshipped. The spies were watching. They rushed back to King Darius and told him about Daniel's behaviour. The king now had to send for

Daniel and punish him. King Darius knew that he had been tricked, and when he sent Daniel away, he said to him, "Your own God whom you serve will save you." (Daniel 6: 16)

Daniel was taken and thrown into a den of lions. No one was allowed to go near the den until the following day. That night King Darius could not sleep. He knew he had been wrong to punish Daniel, who was a good man. He would not eat and no one could comfort him. Early the next morning he went to the lions' den. When he got there Darius called out, "Daniel, servant of the living God, has your God been able to save you from the lions?" (Daniel 6: 20) Daniel replied to the king that God had watched over him, and he had sent his angel to shut the mouths of the lions so that they had not harmed him. King Darius was very happy to know that Daniel was unharmed. He knew that the power of God had protected him from the lions and so he sent out a new decree to all his people, telling them that they must worship Daniel's God.

Because he had stood firm in times of great stress and trusted in God to save him, God blessed Daniel, and King Darius made him the second ruler in the kingdom.

Prayers

1   Lord Jesus, whenever we feel afraid, help us to know that you are with us. We know that you are strong, that you love us and you care for us. Make us brave, like Daniel, and help us to put our trust in you. Amen.

2   Dear Lord, may we never be afraid to say and do the things which we know are right. Please keep us faithful to you in all our work and play. Amen.

3   O God, you have made us and you will keep us. We are never alone, for you are always by our side and we are safe with you. Help us to fear nothing, to be brave and always to trust you, through Jesus Christ our Lord. Amen.

Hymns

Praise the Lord, you heavens adore him (CP 35)
All the nations of the earth (CP 14)

~ ~ ~ ~ ~ ~ ~ ~ ~ ~ ~ ~

D is for Daring
William Tell

I am sure you can think of many acts of daring: the pilots who flew the first aeroplanes, sailors who have travelled round the world by themselves, explorers who have discovered new continents, mountaineers who have climbed very high mountains. If we turn on the radio, watch the television or read newspapers we learn of more acts of daring every day and sometimes we say, "I don't know how he could have dared." We admire people who seem so fearless in the face of great danger.

Today's story is a very old one, about a man called William Tell who lived in Switzerland. Switzerland was ruled in those days by Austria, and one of the attendants of the Austrian Duke was Gessler. Gessler enjoyed the power he had over the Swiss people. He had a nasty, cruel streak in his nature.

He hated William Tell, for William was fearless and often disobeyed Gessler's laws. Gessler was determined that one day he would make William Tell pay for this and he thought up a clever plan. He found a cap which had the badge of the Austrian king sewn on it. He put it on a stake in the village square and told the Swiss people that they must bow to it whenever they passed. William Tell was up in the mountains looking after the cattle, when the order was given. He did not know of Gessler's new rule and if he had, it is unlikely that he would have obeyed.

One day William returned to the village. He walked through the square and at once Gessler pounced upon him for not bowing as he passed by the cap. William Tell was angry and he refused to bow to a cap, just to please the pompous Gessler. Gessler decided to take William Tell and his young son prisoner and he ordered them both to him. They approached him fearlessly. Then Gessler noticed the bow and arrows that William carried and he thought of something even more cruel. Gessler told William to place an apple on the top of his head, then shoot the apple from his son's head with his arrow. If he succeeded they would both be free. If not, they would both die.

William Tell begged Gessler to change his mind, for, brave as he was, he dreaded hurting his own child.

26

However, his son, with great daring, stood up and said in a clear voice, "Don't worry, father, I'll take my place. I know your arrow will not miss its target." The apple was placed on his head. William Tell took aim. The arrow flew through the air and the apple was split in half. Not a hair on the boy's head was harmed.

Gessler's plan had failed. Then William pointed out to Gessler the second arrow he had at hand. "If my son had been injured," he told him, "that second arrow was for you."

Let us make sure that we do not cause others to suffer through any actions of ours. Let us be daring, adventurous and curious as we go through life. But let us, too, be sure that when we are daring we are justified in what we do.

Prayers

1   Help us, God, to be brave, to be daring and to do the right thing whenever we are faced with evil. Amen.

2   Lord Jesus, whenever we feel full of fear help us to be brave. Make us remember that you are always near to us ready to help us and protect us. Teach us to trust you and give us the grace to support others in their fears as you support each one of us. Amen.

3   We pray for courage. Courage to help others when they are in danger. Courage to help ourselves when we are afraid. Courage always to do what we think is right. Help us to live brave and cheerful lives, to dare all for the sake of Jesus Christ, our Lord. Amen.

Hymns

When a knight won his spurs (WCV 66)
He who would valiant be (WCV 40)

~ ~ ~ ~ ~ ~ ~ ~ ~ ~ ~ ~ ~

D is for David the Shepherd

Psalm 23

Long before Jesus was born, there lived in Bethlehem a farmer who owned a lot of land. He had many vineyards, big beautiful fields to harvest and a large flock of sheep that had to be looked after. The name of the farmer was

Jesse and he had eight sons. All his sons helped him on the farm and as he grew older, they did more and more of the work. In time the oldest sons went off to join King Saul's army. By this time David, the youngest, was old enough to help.

David's job was to care for the sheep and he was very conscientious about it. David learned to be a good shepherd. He knew what might harm the sheep and he tried to keep them safe. David knew where the streams were where his sheep could drink safely. He learnt how to use the tools of his trade skillfully. He had a sling which he used to aim stones at any wild animals that threatened his sheep. At other times he would use the sling to send a stone through the air to frighten a wandering sheep and bring it running back to the flock. He got used to being on his own. He would roam the hillsides with his shepherd's crook which he used to free sheep caught in the brambles or on the ledges of a cliff.

He was happy and contented and often he would sing as he sat on the green hillsides watching his sheep. David could play the harp and he had plenty of time to practise and to make up new tunes and songs. He made up many songs in praise of God. Some of them have been written down for us and we still sing them today. One of the best known and loved of the songs of David is Psalm 23. In this psalm he says God's care for us is like a shepherd's for his sheep. It begins like this:

> The Lord is my shepherd, I shall want nothing. He makes me to lie down in green pastures, and he leads me beside the waters of peace; he renews life within me, and for his name's sake, guides me in the right path. Even though I walk through the valley dark as death I fear no evil for thou art with me, Thy staff and thy crook are my comfort. (Psalm 23: 1–4)

David is anointed by Samuel

David cannot have known then of the great plans God had for him. But God spoke to the prophet Samuel and told him that the king to follow Saul was to be chosen from the sons of Jesse. Samuel was to go to Jesse's house and anoint the new king. (1 Samuel 16: 1–4) God promised he would show Samuel which of Jesse's sons he had chosen.

Samuel was welcomed by Jesse and Samuel blessed him. Then each of Jesse's sons in turn was presented to Samuel, but not one of these did God choose. Samuel asked Jesse whether he had any more sons and Jesse replied that there was only David, the youngest, who was out with the sheep. Samuel insisted that David be sent for and when he was presented to Samuel the Lord said, "Rise and anoint him, this is the man." And the Bible tells us that Samuel "took the horn of oil and anointed him in the presence of his brothers. Then the spirit of the Lord came upon David and was with him from that day onwards."

David did not immediately become king, but some time after he had been anointed by Samuel, Saul sent for him. Saul was old and ill, and he wished to be soothed and comforted by hearing the sweet music which David played on his harp. David went to Saul, and Saul was pleased with him and grew to love him. He asked David to stay with him. Whenever Saul was unhappy, David would take his harp and play it, and Saul would become peaceful. (1 Samuel 16: 22–23)

We can read much more about the life of David in the books of Samuel in the Bible.

Prayers

1 O God we thank you for David, the shepherd boy of Bethlehem, who showed us that whatever work we are chosen to do we should always do it well that we may please you in all our ways. Amen.

2 Dear Lord, give us pleasure in all the simple things of life, so that we take time to enjoy the beauty of your wonderful creation and praise you for your glorious works as did David on the hillside of Bethlehem so long ago. Amen.

3 You, Lord, will light my candle. You, Lord, will make my darkness to be bright. O send forth your light and your truth that they may lead me, and bring me to your holy hill and to your dwelling. Amen.

Hymns

The God of love my shepherd is (WCV 36)
Lord of all power, I give you my will (100 HT 62)

~ ~ ~ ~ ~ ~ ~ ~ ~ ~ ~ ~

D is for St David

The healing of Paulinus

There are many stories told about David, the patron saint of Wales, whose special day is on 1 March. On this day the wild daffodils are said to open their buds and this flower is the emblem of the Welsh people. Many people in Wales wear either daffodils or leeks in their button-holes on 1 March.

David was born in Wales. He loved his native land very much and wanted to be a good servant to the people. When he was a boy he was taught in a monastery, where he learned to love God. He was taught the scriptures by monks who were devoted to God's work. David decided that he would be a priest one day and so he worked very hard.

David knew that God had chosen him for a special purpose and given him special gifts and talents to use in his service. When David was still young and studying at the monastery, there was there an old monk called Paulinus who was going blind. Paulinus longed to see the beautiful daffodils that bloomed in the gardens of the monastery in the spring once again. He prayed to God that his sight might come back, and when he prayed he heard a voice answering his prayers and telling him to allow the boy David to touch his eyes. Paulinus sent for David and asked him to put his fingers on his eyes. David did, and Paulinus was able to see again.

The preaching of David

David became a priest and he travelled around Wales preaching to the people. In one place the crowds were so big and the winds were so strong that the people could not hear the voice of the bishop who was speaking to them. Someone then said that David should speak and that everyone would hear him. They called David forward. David prayed to God to give him the strength to find the right words to say. As he stood up to speak, the ground beneath him rose so that he stood higher than the crowd. All the people could hear him clearly.

David founded his own monastery in Wales. There the monks lived simply and worked hard. They grew all their own food and did all their own work on the land and in the monastery. Although the monks lived very simply, they always welcomed anyone who came in need of help. David was a true disciple of Jesus and served him all his life by working for others. Later he was made Archbishop of Wales.

Today in Wales there is a beautiful cathedral in memory of David, the patron saint. The place is called St David's and is the smallest city in the British Isles. In the cathedral is a small box in which the bones of St David have been preserved. This box is very precious and it is kept locked in a special place and only opened very occasionally. You can see the box if you visit the Cathedral of St David in Pembrokeshire.

Prayers

1 As we think today about St David, let us remember how he thought of others and tried always to serve God through his actions. Let us pray that we, too, may be good disciples. We ask this for Jesus' sake. Amen.

2 O God, you chose your servant David to be the apostle of the Welsh people, so that he could guide them by his example. Grant us to keep the faith which he taught and to follow in his footsteps, through Jesus Christ our Lord. Amen.

3 Almighty and everlasting God, who lit the flame of love in the heart of St David, grant to us the same faith and power of love, that as we remember him this day, we may follow his example, through Jesus Christ our Lord. Amen.

Hymns

Christ is the King, O friends rejoice (100 HT 12)
My faith it is an oaken staff (WCV 55)

~ ~ ~ ~ ~ ~ ~ ~ ~ ~ ~ ~ ~

E is for Easter

The resurrection

Easter is one of the great festivals of the Christian Church. On Easter Sunday we remember how Jesus rose from the dead. The disciples had seen Jesus die and when they saw he was alive again they were certain that all his teaching was true. Joyfully they greeted their Lord and prepared to serve him for the rest of their lives.

After Jesus had died on the Cross his body was placed in the tomb in the garden of Joseph of Arimathea. A large stone was put in front of the entrance. Nobody went to the garden the following day for that was the Sabbath Day. But the next day, now called Easter Sunday, three women went early to the tomb. They had prepared oils and spices to anoint Jesus' body. As they came to the garden they wondered who would move the stone away for them. But when they got close enough to see they discovered that it had already been rolled back. They came nearer to the tomb and found two angels where the body of Jesus had been. (Luke 24: 1–10) The angels told the women that they had nothing to fear. Jesus had been raised from the dead and the women were to go and tell the news to the disciples. The message from Jesus was that he would meet them again in Galilee.

The women ran as fast as they could and went to tell Peter and John, who ran quickly to the garden. Peter went into the tomb and John followed. They found it was empty, just as the women had told them. At that moment they understood what Jesus had meant when he said he would rise from the dead.

Jesus appears to Mary Magdalene

The disciples went back home, but one of the women, Mary Magdalene, was still in the garden. She was crying. She could not bear to leave the place where she had last seen Jesus. She did not understand all that had happened. She felt lonely and unhappy. As she peered again into the tomb, one of the angels said to her, "Why are you weeping?" Mary answered, "They have taken my Lord away and I don't know where they have laid him." Then Mary turned round and she saw Jesus standing there, but through her tears she did not recognise him. Jesus said to her, "Why are you weeping? Who are you looking for?" Mary thought this person must be one of the gardeners and so she said to him, "If it is you, sir, who has removed the body of Jesus, please tell me where you have laid him." Jesus spoke just one word. He said "Mary", and she immediately knew who it was. She knelt at his feet and said, "My master." Jesus then told Mary to go back to the other disciples and tell them the good news. Mary went with her glad message and said to them, "I have seen the Lord." (John 20: 10–18)

Prayers

1 Jesus, our Lord, we praise you that nothing could keep you dead in the grave. You are stronger than death itself. Help us to remember that we have nothing to fear because you are alive and by our side. Amen.

2 We thank you Lord Jesus that springtime reminds us of the first Easter Day, when you rose again to be with us always, and to bring new life and joy every day. Give to us and to all those we love the joy of Easter in our hearts and the living power of your presence in our lives. Amen.

3 Jesus, stand among us
In your risen power,
Let this time of worship
Be a hallowed hour.

Bid the fears and sorrows
From each one depart,
Breathe your Holy Spirit
Into every heart. Amen.

Hymns

When Jesus walked in Galilee (CP 25)
Jesus, humble was your birth (100 HT 46)

~ ~ ~ ~ ~ ~ ~ ~ ~ ~ ~ ~

E is for Elijah

Elijah is fed by ravens

Elijah lived in a land where there was little rain, and sometimes little food as the crops would not grow. God warned Elijah that a long drought was coming and he guided him to a place where he would be able to drink from a stream. God promised Elijah that he would send ravens with food for him, and every morning and evening the birds brought bread and meat. (1 Kings 17: 2–8) After a while the stream dried up and God spoke again to Elijah. He told him to go to a certain village where he would find a widow who would look after him.

When Elijah reached the village he saw the poor widow, who was gathering sticks. (1 Kings 16: 10–16) He asked her for a little water to drink and she brought him some. Then Elijah said he would like a little bread to eat as well. The poor woman replied that she had only a handful of flour in a jar and a little oil in a flask. She had hardly enough to make bread for herself and her little boy. She was quite desperate. Elijah told the widow not to be afraid. God, he said, was guiding him and that if the woman first made him a little cake, she would be able to cook something for herself and her son as well. The woman listened to Elijah and did as he asked. He said to her, "The jar of flour shall not give out, nor the flask of oil fail, until the Lord sends rain on the land." These words proved to be true. Although the woman cooked for him and her family for a long time she always had enough oil and flour for all their needs.

Elijah brings the widow's son back to life

Later a sad thing happened to the poor widow who had helped Elijah. Her little boy died. She was very unhappy and she blamed Elijah for what had happened. Elijah felt sorry for his friend who had helped him when he was hungry and thirsty and he said to the woman, "Give your son to me." (1 Kings 16: 17–24) Then Elijah carried the little boy up to the flat roof on top of the house and put him down on his own bed. Elijah prayed very hard to God to help him. Then he breathed deeply on the child and called out to God, saying, "O Lord my God, let the breath of life return to the body of this child." God heard and answered Elijah's prayer and the boy began to breathe again. Elijah lifted the boy up gently and carried him back to his mother. He said to her, "Look, your son is alive." She was overjoyed and said, "Now I know for certain that you are a man of God and that the word of the Lord on your lips is truth."

Prayers

1   Dear God, as we read the stories of the prophets of old, we are reminded how great was the faith of those who believed and trusted in you. Help us to grow in faith day by day and always to put our trust in you. Amen.

2   Thank you God that you care for us all. We know that every day you will provide for all our needs and that you will give us each day our daily bread even as you gave bread and water to Elijah. Amen.

3   O God, we thank you for the lives of all the great men and women who have gone before us. We thank you for Elijah and the prophets who put all their faith in you. We thank you that the events of their lives have been recorded so that we can learn from them. Amen.

Hymns

O God, thou art the father (WCV 122)
Holy spirit hear us (WCV 29)

~ ~ ~ ~ ~ ~ ~ ~ ~ ~ ~ ~ ~

E is for Enlightenment
Prince Siddhartha

Many hundreds of years ago, a young prince called Siddhartha lived at the foot of the mountains of the Himalayas. When he was born, his father asked the fortune-tellers to say what would happen to Siddhartha when he grew up. The prince's father expected that he would have a life of luxury and be an important ruler. So Siddhartha's father was very upset when the fortune-tellers said that his son would leave home to help all the suffering people in the world. Siddhartha's father decided

35

that the best way to make sure that his son always stayed at home was to keep him inside the walls of the palace. The people in charge of the young prince had to make sure that his days were filled with happiness and that he never saw anything or anyone that could make him unhappy. But when Siddhartha was a young man he wanted to explore beyond the palace grounds and he asked his father if he might visit the park. His father agreed, but first he sent his servants ahead, so that they could make sure that the prince would see nothing which would upset him.

The visit passed successfully, but on his way home, a very old man crossed the road in front of the carriage in which the prince was riding. Siddhartha was amazed. He had never seen an old person before. The bent back, the slow walk, the wrinkled skin of the old man made him feel very perplexed. "What is wrong with this man?", he asked his servants. They told the prince that the stranger was old. The prince asked more questions, "Could anyone grow old?" "Would he himself grow old one day?" Prince Siddhartha was filled with horror when he learned the awful truth. Old age, sickness and death come to everyone. The prince had never seen the suffering of other people before, but now he learned the truth. Most people have hardship, suffering and grief in their lives.

Siddhartha decided he must leave the palace. And so, one night, he stealthily crept away, never to return. The young prince gave up his rich clothes. He lived a life of poverty and went without food for long periods of time. But although he tried hard to find out, he could not discover why people must suffer.

Finally he sat down under a tree and made up his mind that he would think and think until he found the answer. Finally the answer came to him. Siddhartha decided that people's suffering was because of selfishness. he discovered that the secret of happiness was helping others and loving all living things. From that moment Siddhartha became known as Buddha, the enlightened one. The tree under which he had sat when this knowledge dawned upon him was called the Bodhi tree, the tree of enlightenment.

The Buddha never thought himself to be a god, but people who followed him built temples in his name and worshipped him. Now Buddhists celebrate the feast of Vesak. On this day in May, Buddha is said to have been born and died. It is also the day when Siddhartha is supposed to have gained enlightenment beneath the Bodhi tree.

We, too, would do well to remember the teachings of Buddha, for we know that Jesus himself came to help and serve others, to show all men the way to the kingdom of heaven. Jesus, too, showed us his love and concern for all living things. Even the sparrows that fall to the ground are known to God, our Father in heaven.

Prayers

1   The Buddha said,
        Overcome anger by love,
        Overcome evil by doing good,
        Overcome greed by being generous,
        Overcome lies by telling the truth.
    Let us remember the life of the Buddha, and, like him, live simply and help others. Amen.

2   Dear Lord Jesus, as we grow up and learn to follow the wonderful example that you have set before us, teach us to learn tolerance and understanding. Help us to use the knowledge we gain to benefit other people and to follow where you would lead us. Amen.

3   O God, our Father, grant us
    The love which is always ready to forgive;
    The love which is always eager to help;
    The love which is always happier to give than to get.
    And so grant that living in love,
    We may live like Jesus. Amen.

Hymns

I belong to a family (SM 7)
Far round the world thy children sing their song (WCV 71)

~ ~ ~ ~ ~ ~ ~ ~ ~ ~ ~ ~ ~

E is for Epiphany
The three kings

The feast of the Epiphany is on 6 January and at this time we remember how the wise men from the East brought their gifts to Jesus. The wise men followed the new star which shone in the sky and guided them on their way. It showed them the way to Bethlehem in Judaea where the new king was born.

The kings from the East did not know exactly where Jesus was, so they went to the palace of King Herod at Jerusalem to ask him. King Herod could not tell them, but he was very disturbed by what the wise men said. Herod feared that if there was a new king in Judaea he might lose his throne. But Herod was very clever. He pretended that he, too, wanted to worship the new king. So he told the wise men to return to him when they had found the baby. But Herod did not intend to worship him. He wanted to find out all he could about this new prince, so that he could put an end to his life. Then the new king would not be able to threaten his own position.

The three wise men left the palace and continued their journey. The star continued to guide them until they reached the place where the baby was. (Matthew 2: 10–12)

The legend of Babushka

Many legends have grown up around the visit of the three wise men to Bethlehem. One is an old Russian story about a woman called Babushka. We are told that on their way to Jerusalem the wise men stopped at the home of Babushka for a rest. Babushka listened fascinated, to what the three kings told her about the birth of the new king. Babushka said that she, too, would like more than anything else to go and worship the baby. Caspar, Melchior and Balthasar encouraged her to go with them, but they were anxious to leave that night as they had to follow the star which had been sent to guide them on their way.

Although Babushka very much wanted to go she delayed getting ready, and so the kings set off without her. Much later Babushka closed the door of her house, ready at last to follow the wise men. But there was no sign of Caspar, Melchior or Balthasar. They had gone on their way long since. Babushka kept looking for the way and asking for guidance, but no one could direct her and she could not find the right road to Bethlehem. She never found the baby because she hesitated too long. But Russian children believe that every Christmas she sets out with her gifts for the baby. She looks into every house and wherever she finds there are children, she leaves a present for each one, in case one of them should be the baby she is looking for. When Russian children wake on Christmas morning they look to see whether Babushka has been, just as you look to see if Father Christmas has remembered you.

Prayers

1   O Lord Jesus Christ, who by the shining of a star showed yourself to those who looked for you, show us your heavenly light from day to day, and give us strength fo follow till we find you. Amen.

2   O Lord Jesus Christ to whom the wise men brought their gifts, myrrh for sorrow, frankincense for joy and gold for kingliness, we offer to you now our joys and sorrows, and all our hopefulness and growing strength. We offer you our lives. Please take them, Lord, and make them more like yours. Amen.

3   To Jesus, now the infant king,
    The wise men came, their gifts to bring,
    Like them, we now before you lay
    Our humble gift of love today.
    O show us, Lord, what we can do
    That we may know and serve you too. Amen.

Hymns

As with gladness men of old (WCV 106)
Wise men seeking Jesus (SM 17)

~ ~ ~ ~ ~ ~ ~ ~ ~ ~ ~ ~

F is for Fear

Peter walks on water

There are times when all of us feel afraid. When we feel like this we want someone to be with us, to help us to get over our fear. Some people are afraid of spiders, others are afraid of the dark. Some people don't like being on their own and some are afraid of new work that they don't understand straight away. We all have to try to get over our fears. We don't have to be ashamed of them but we have to try to be brave enough to face them. All this is much easier to do if we remember that we are never on our own. Jesus is close to us, and he will help us and be with us if we turn to him and trust him.

Jesus knew what it was like to be afraid. Before his enemies took him away to put him to death on the cross he prayed to his father in Heaven and asked him to give him the strength to do God's will. His friends were very much afraid that week in Jerusalem. Peter lost his nerve completely and pretended he didn't know Jesus at all. On Easter Sunday evening when Jesus came to them the disciples were sitting in a locked room, because they were afraid of being arrested. There are many times in the Bible when we read of people being afraid. At the very beginning of the Bible we read how Adam and Eve were afraid to meet God in the Garden of Eden after they had disobeyed him and eaten the forbidden fruit. One of the stories is about St Peter, and it reminds us that many of our fears disappear if we trust in Jesus' power to help us.

After Jesus had fed the 5,000 people with the five loaves and two fishes, he sent the disciples on ahead of him. He stayed behind to send all the crowds of people back to their own homes. (Matthew 14: 22–23) When it was quiet again, Jesus went up the hillside to pray. He was all by himself. The disciples had taken the boat and they were well out to sea when it became quite stormy. There was a strong wind and the sea was rough. Very early in the morning Jesus came towards them, walking on the waters of the lake. The disciples were terrified when they looked over the side of the boat and saw this person walking towards them. They cried out in terror and they said, "It is a ghost." But Jesus spoke to them. He said, "Take heart. It's me. Do not be afraid." Peter at once called back, "Lord, if it is really you, tell me to come to you over the water." Jesus said, "Come" and Peter stepped down from the boat, and walked over the water towards Jesus. Suddenly Peter realised how stormy the weather was. He was amazed that he was actually walking on the water. He became frightened and began to sink. He shouted out to Jesus, "Save me, Lord," and Jesus reached out and caught hold of him. Jesus said to Peter, "Why did you hesitate? While you had faith you could walk in safety, but your faith became weak and so you started to sink." As they climbed into the boat the other disciples knelt at Jesus' feet and said, "Truly you are the Son of God."

Let us ask Jesus to make us brave and help us to overcome all our fears as we put our trust in him.

Prayers

1   Jesus, when we are afraid, help us to remember that you are with us, nearer than our breathing, closer than our beating hearts. You understand our fears better than we do, so let us trust in you. Give us the grace to support others in their fears, as you support each of us. Amen.

2   The King of love my shepherd is,
    Whose goodness faileth never,
    I nothing lack if I am his
    And he is mine for ever. Amen.

3   Lord Jesus, help us never to be afraid, and give us strength to go on in times of difficulty. Help us to remember that you are always by our side and that we are safe with you. Amen.

Hymns

Think of all the things we lose (CP 57)
Would you walk by on the other side (CP 70)

~ ~ ~ ~ ~ ~ ~ ~ ~ ~ ~ ~

F is for Fire

Elijah and the worshippers of Baal

You all know that fire can be dangerous. That is why you are told not to play with matches and to be very careful with fireworks. But fire is very important to us. We use it

41

for heating and cooking and we are glad of its warmth and the comfort it can bring.

There is a strange story in the Bible about the prophet Elijah. (1 Kings 18: 21–39) He was very worried because the people were turning away from the one true God and worshipping idols and images. Many people were worshipping a God they called Baal. Elijah knew this was wrong and he tried to bring the people back to God but they would not listen to him. Elijah knew he would have to do something to show the people their mistake. So he said to the people who worshipped Baal, "We must prove who is the one true God. You prepare an altar for Baal, and I shall prepare an altar for God. We shall each offer a similar sacrifice and ask our own God to set fire to the sacrifice to show that he hears our prayers." The people cheered as they listened to Elijah's words. They thought this was a splendid idea.

Elijah told the leaders of Baal that they should go first. He told them to choose their bull and to put it on the altar without setting fire to it. They did this and then they began to call to Baal to send down fire to light the sacrifice on their altar. All morning they called out, "Baal, Baal, answer us," but nothing happened. They began to chant louder and to dance around their altar. Elijah called out to them, "Shout louder, Baal does not hear you. Perhaps he is deep in thought or perhaps he has gone to sleep. Maybe he has gone away somewhere." So the people who worshipped Baal kept on calling to their god, still nothing happened.

Next it was Elijah's turn. He took twelve stones to build his altar. He then prepared his sacrifice and laid it on the altar for the Lord God. Then Elijah did a very strange thing. He said to the people who were helping him, "Fill four jars with water." They did this and then Elijah made them pour the water over the altar. Again he told them to fill their jars with water and pour the water over the altar. Then a third time, he insisted that they fill the water jars and pour the water on the altar. Then Elijah came forward. He began to pray, saying, "Lord God let it be known today that you are God in Israel and that I, your servant, have done all these things at your command. Answer me, O Lord, answer me and let the people know that you, Lord, are God."

And then the fire began to burn. It burnt all round the altar and the people saw what was happening. Then they knelt on the ground and they cried, "The Lord is God. The Lord is God."

So the people turned back to God gain. They listened to Elijah because they understood that he was a prophet sent by God to show them the right way. And the Lord God continued to guide Elijah and Elijah prayed to God to help him with his work.

Prayers

1   O God we thank you for your gift of fire which brings us warmth and comfort. Help us to use all your gifts in the right way and always to give thanks to you, the one true God. Amen.

2   O God, we know how great and wonderful you are. We ask you to strengthen our faith that we may believe in you with greater understanding day by day. Help us to realise that we do not need more proof of your care because you have already provided for all our needs. Amen.

3   *Prayer of St Francis*
    Praised be our Lord for our Brother Sun
    That caused all day his course to run.
    For our Sister Moon, praised be the Lord
    By Stars in heavenly hosts adored.
    For our Brothers, the Wind, the Cloud and the Air
    Whose blessings all your creatures share.
    Praised be our Lord for Waters bright,
    For our Brother Fire, his warmth and light,
    To Mother Earth, your gifts you send,
    O God our Father and our Friend. Amen.

Hymns

All creatures of our God and King (WCV 8)
Colours of day, dawn into the mind (CP 55)

~ ~ ~ ~ ~ ~ ~ ~ ~ ~ ~ ~ ~

F is for Forgiveness
The parable of the prodigal son

Jesus taught us that we must forgive each other. We must forgive people, not just our friends, but our enemies as well. We have to forgive people who are being deliberately unkind to us. Jesus forgave his enemies. When the soldiers were nailing him to the cross, hammering the nails through his hands and his feet, the only words that Jesus spoke were, "Father, forgive them, they do not know what they are doing." (Luke 23: 34) That was the example that Jesus set for us in his own life.

Jesus also told the people parables about forgiveness. One of these stories was about a father who had two sons. (Luke 15: 11–32) The father had a lot of money and his younger son went to him and asked if he could have the part of the money which would be his one day. His father was a generous man, so he divided his money between his two sons. The older boy stayed at home and continued to help his father with the farm, but the younger one went off to have a good time. He went to a new town and made new friends. He didn't bother to work. He just enjoyed himself because he had plenty of money for all that he needed: food, drink, presents and parties. But money is quickly wasted, and one day the younger son realised he wasn't well off any more. he gave fewer parties and many of his new friends began to leave him.

At just about the same time there was a terrible famine in that country. Food would not grow because there was no rain, and it became very expensive. The young man began to feel hungry. He no longer had enough money to buy the food he needed. Eventually he managed to find a job looking after somebody's pigs and some days he felt so hungry he wanted to eat the scraps that had been thrown out for them. One day when he was out with the pigs he thought about his home, his father and his brother. He felt very sorry that he had decided to leave home and enjoy life on his own. Nothing had worked out the way he had expected it to and he wanted to go back to his father and tell him he was sorry. He knew it would not be an easy thing to do, for he had wasted his father's hard-earned money and he felt sure he would be very angry with him.

44

So the younger son decided that if he went back to his father's house he would ask his father to accept him as a servant and not as his son any more. He knew he would still be better off, for his father's servants always had enough to eat.

He began the journey home, wondering what sort of reception he would get. But before he reached the house his father saw him coming. The sight of his son returning home gladdened the father's heart and he ran out to meet him and put his arm around his son and kissed him. And the younger son said to him, "Father, I am sorry. I have sinned against God and against you. I am no longer fit to be called your son." But the father said to his servants, "Quick! Fetch a robe, my best one, and put it on him. Put a ring on his finger and shoes on his feet. Bring the fatted calf and kill it and let us have a feast to celebrate this day. For this son of mine was dead and has come back to life; he was lost and is found."

The older of the two boys was still out working on the farm when the party started. He did not know his brother had come home. He heard all the music and dancing and he wondered what was going on. One of the servants told him what had happened and the older boy felt cross and jealous. He refused to go into the house and join in with the celebrations and his father came out to talk to him to see what had gone wrong. Then the older boy said to his father in an angry voice, "You have never given a party for me, but I am the one who has stayed at home and helped you all these years. I have not disobeyed you and wasted your money like my brother has done. Why should you seem so pleased to see him again?". And the father said to his son, "My boy, you are always with me, and everything I have is yours. How could we help celebrating this happy day? Your brother was dead and has come back to life. He was lost and is found." So the father helped his son to forgive his younger brother.

And Jesus explained that just as the father in the story was able to forgive his children, so our heavenly Father will forgive us. No matter what wrong we have done, if he knows that we are truly sorry, he will forgive us and comfort us with his love.

Prayers

1   Loving Father, sometimes we do things that we know
    are wrong. Help us to be truly sorry and forgive us.
    May we always remember your great love for us.
    Amen.

2   Our Father in Heaven, please forgive us for the
    wrongs we have done. For bad temper and angry
    words, for being greedy and wanting the best for
    ourselves, for making other people unhappy. Please
    forgive us, Heavenly Father. Amen.

3   O God our Heavenly Father, forgive us for all our
    faults remembered and forgotten. For the things we
    ought to have done and have not done; for the things
    we have done which have brought sorrow to ourselves
    and to others. And as we pray, ourselves, to be
    forgiven, help us to forgive those who have done
    wrong to us, through Jesus Christ our Lord. Amen.

Hymns

Father lead me day by day (WCV 27)
There is a green hill far away (WCV 110)

~ ~ ~ ~ ~ ~ ~ ~ ~ ~ ~ ~ ~

F is for Fortitude
The life of Helen Keller

Another word for fortitude is strength: not physical
strength but inner strength. It is what makes people keep
on trying even when there are great difficulties. It is
accepting all kinds of problems and having the courage to
make the best of one's life no matter what has gone
wrong. A person who has great fortitude is a person with
strength of character and courage, a person we can admire
very much.

One such person was Helen Keller. Helen was born as a
perfectly normal baby but when she was still very tiny she
caught a fever. She was so ill she almost died, but her
parents nursed her and she began to get better. But the
fever left her both blind and deaf. Because she was deaf
she became dumb as well. Nobody could communicate
with Helen. She could not see, she could not hear, she

could not speak. Her parents could not even tell Helen they loved her and know that she would understand. They did all they could to make life bearable for her. They washed her, they fed her, they helped her to walk but they did not know how to control her when she flew into terrible rages. We can understand why Helen got so upset. She could never tell anyone what she wanted or how she felt. She couldn't even see the people who tried to help her, so she became very wild. She bit, she scratched, she kicked. She did the only things possible for her to let others know she was not happy.

Helen's parents were near to despair. They did not know what they could do. Then a person called Anne Sullivan came into their lives. Anne came to their home as Helen's teacher. She had been specially trained to teach blind children, although she had never met a child with so many handicaps as Helen. Anne felt sorry for Helen, but she knew that if she was to help, she would first have to tame Helen. So because she loved her, Anne was very firm with Helen. Whenever Helen scratched or bit or kicked, Anne did the same back to her. It sounds cruel, but it was the only way Helen could realise what her own behaviour was like.

At first Helen resented Anne, but Anne was loving too. She showed Helen how much she cared for her by stroking her gently and cuddling her. She kissed her and comforted her and gradually Helen came to realise that Anne was her true friend. Once Anne had gained Helen's confidence she was able to begin the task of trying to teach this blind, deaf and dumb child. There was only one way to start and that was through feeling. Anne began to teach Helen the deaf and dumb alphabet, by feeling letters on the palms of her hand. It is hard for deaf and dumb people to learn this language, even if they can see. For Helen everything was much more difficult. But as soon as she realised she was going to be able to communicate with people, Helen worked and worked until she had mastered every letter. Anne was amazed how quickly Helen learnt. She discovered that locked away in Helen's dark, silent world, there was a really clever little girl. Helen responded to all that Anne gave her. She learnt Braille, the reading language of the blind. Then Anne began teaching Helen to talk.

Helen persevered and showed great fortitude. How easy it would have been for her to give up. But she did not stop. When she was twelve years old she wrote her first story. Later, when she was old enough, she went to college and Anne went with her, helping her to translate the lectures into finger language. Anne, too, had great fortitude and perseverance. What a wonderful team the two of them must have made as they worked together and what an inspiration to everyone else around.

Prayers

1　O God, when we are faced with tasks we find difficult, help us never to give up. May we remember the lives of many of your servants who have shown great fortitude and help us to be like them. Amen.

2　We thank you Lord Jesus for eyes to see, ears to hear and lips with which to speak. Please bless all those who are not able to see or to hear or to speak. Give them courage and fortitude to persevere in the face of difficulties. Amen.

3　Eyes to see and ears to hear
God's good gifts to me and you,
Eyes and ears he gave to us
To help each other the whole day through.

Minds to think and hearts to love
God's good gifts to me and you,
Minds and hearts he gave to us
To help each other the whole day through. Amen.

Hymns

Through the night of doubt and sorrow (WCV 53)
My faith it is an oaken staff (WCV 55)

~ ~ ~ ~ ~ ~ ~ ~ ~ ~ ~ ~

G is for Gandhi

Hinduism

Many Indian people are Hindus and they practise a faith which is different from ours. The people have many gods. All these gods are worshipped but the same spirit is in all of them. There are two main rules which the Hindus have to obey. The first is that they must always seek the truth and the second that they must not harm anyone or anything. Because of the second rule, the Hindus try to avoid causing death or destruction. Some Hindus have even been known to brush paths before they walk down them, in order to avoid treading on an ant or another tiny creature.

The Hindus have followed many great leaders and they have many festivals and customs. Some of them may seem strange to us because we do not know as much about them as we do about our own special occasions. When we have holidays to celebrate Christmas or Easter, we remember the special events in the life of Jesus Christ. The Hindus celebrate their special religious days with festivals and dancing. There are many stories and legends about the Hindu gods, but today we are going to think especially about one very great man, a Hindu, who you have probably heard of.

Gandhi

Mahatma Gandhi trained as a lawyer and was an important man among his own circle of business friends. He married and had children of his own. For a time he went to work in South Africa and there he was horrified at the way Asian people were treated. Gandhi fought for justice and a better life for his own people in Africa. Those in authority found him a nuisance. More than once Gandhi was sent to prison. But Gandhi continued to fight for his people even though there were so many difficulties. All through the troubled times, he never forgot the Hindu rule of harmlessness. Gandhi never carried weapons. He never injured another man. Many people followed him, but Gandhi knew that only men of peace could help their cause.

When Gandhi returned to India, the country was

49

governed by Britain. Gandhi felt that the time was right for the British people to leave India and let the Indians rule their own land. The British did not want to lose power, but Gandhi had a lot of support from his own people. They followed his example and whenever they could they argued their right to govern their own country. Many Indians died for the cause but Gandhi would not accept the use of violence by his own people. When he heard that there were riots among the Indian people he showed his disapproval by refusing food. Twice Gandhi starved himself almost to death. He refused to eat when he knew his own people were fighting in India. Because Gandhi was so much loved by his followers they stopped rioting.

But Gandhi himself died in a violent way. He was shot by a man who did not believe that Gandhi's example of peaceful resistance was the right way. And so the life of a very great man came to a sad end.

Prayers

1 O Lord, may we feel that you are the soul of our soul, may our bodies be your home, and may everything we enjoy be an offering to you: may you rule our lives, may our every word by a hymn to you, our every act your adoration. May we see the whole world as lighted by your light and may we come to know you more and more each day. Amen.

2 I pray not for wealth,
   I pray not for honours,
   I pray not for pleasures,
   I only pray that all through my life
   I may have love:
   That I may have love, to love thee. Amen.

3 Let the earth and the water,
   The air and the fruits of my country,
   Be sweet, my God.
   Let the promises and the hopes,
   The deeds and the words of my country,
   Be true, my God,
   Let the homes and the markets,
   The forests and the fields of my country,
   Be full, my God,

Let the lives and the hearts,
Of the peoples of my country,
Be one, my God. Amen.

Hymns

They say he's wonderful (SM 49)
Blessed are the pure in heart (WCV 44)

~ ~ ~ ~ ~ ~ ~ ~ ~ ~ ~ ~ ~

G is for Garden

The Gardens of Eden and Gethsemane

Many of you are lucky enough to live in a house with a garden. It is lovely to have a garden because you can play outside safely without having to worry about the traffic and your parents know where you are.

In the very first book of the Bible we can read about the first garden that God made. This garden was called the Garden of Eden and it was very beautiful. We are told that "The Lord God made trees spring from the ground, all trees pleasant to look at and good for food, and in the middle of the garden he set the tree of life and the tree of knowledge. There was a river flowing from Eden to water the garden." (Genesis 2: 8–10) He then made man to live in his garden. The first man he named Adam and the first woman was called Eve. He told the man he could eat from every tree in the garden except for the tree of knowledge. When Adam and Eve disobeyed God, He sent them away from the beautiful garden and sent an angel to keep watch over it so that Adam and Eve would not be able to return.

The Garden of Eden is not the only garden that we can read about in the Bible. The Garden of Gethsemane was the place where Jesus went to pray after he had eaten the Last Supper with his friends. It was in this garden that Judas kissed Jesus and betrayed him to his enemies.

After the death of Jesus on the Cross on Good Friday, his friends asked if they could take his body so that they could bury it. When they had got permission, they took Jesus to the tomb in the garden of Joseph of Arimethaea. It was to this garden that the women and the disciples came that joyful Easter morning when they discovered that the stone had been rolled away from the entrance to the tomb. It was in this garden that Mary Magdalene became the first person to see Jesus after he had been raised from the dead.

Gardens are peaceful places and places of beauty. As we think about our own gardens, let us remember some of the experiences of joy and sadness of Jesus and his friends, the disciples, when they visited the garden of Joseph and the Garden of Gethsemane.

Prayers

1   O God, you have made so many beautiful things for us to enjoy. We thank you for our homes and for our gardens. Thank you for the beauty which we see all around us. Amen.

2   Father God, when you made the first garden, you made man, also, to care for the garden you had created. Make us useful helpers, so that we may do our share to keep beautiful the flowers, the plants and the trees for which we are responsible. Amen.

3   God who made the grass,
    The flower, the fruit, the tree,
    The day and night to pass,
    Careth for me. Amen.

4   The kiss of the sun for pardon,
    The song of the birds for mirth,
    One is nearer God's heart in a garden
    Than anywhere else on earth. Amen.

Hymns

A little child may know (WCV 79)
In our dear Lord's garden (WCV 80)

~ ~ ~ ~ ~ ~ ~ ~ ~ ~ ~ ~ ~

G is for Garments

Joseph's coat

As I look at you all I can see how well dressed you are. How well cared for you are. What smart jumpers and cardigans and skirts and trousers and ties you have. What good strong shoes and sandals you have for your feet, and you have got boots for wet weather and plimsolls to change into when you need them. You have macs and coats and anoraks as well as gloves, hats and scarves. And what about your slippers and dressing-gowns, your pyjamas and night-dresses. Aren't we lucky that we have a choice about what we wear?

In some parts of the world, there are children who are not warm enough, whose clothes are ragged and torn and who have no shoes for their feet. So we should not take our lovely clothes for granted but neither should we think too much about them. Jesus said we can worry too much about what we are going to wear and to some of the people who were worrying about unimportant things he said, "Think of the lilies, they neither spin nor weave, yet I tell you, even Solomon in all his splendour was not attired like one of these." (Luke 12: 27)

Many of Jesus' friends were not richly clothed. We know that they were working men and they would have dressed simply according to the job they did. It was a hot country and people usually wore long, loose gowns and they covered their heads to protect them from the burning heat of the sun.

You will all remember the story in the Old Testament about Joseph's special garment. There were twelve boys in Joseph's family. His father was called Jacob and his mother Rachel. When there are a lot of children in the family brothers and sisters very often have to share things. I expect if you have older brothers or sisters you sometimes wear their clothes when they have grown out of them and in the same way some of your things are passed on to your little brothers and sisters when they get too small for you. It was probably the same with the brothers in Joseph's family. Jacob loved Joseph dearly and to show the special place that he had for him in his heart, he made Joseph a special cloak. (Genesis 37: 3) This made the other brothers very jealous.

The coat did not bring Joseph a lot of happiness. Some of his brothers planned to kill him, but Judah said they would do better if they sold Joseph to some rich merchants. They succeeded in doing this and they got twenty pieces of silver for their brother. They also kept Joseph's coat, and because they had to explain to their father why Joseph did not return home, they made up a dreadful story. They tore the coat into pieces and they dipped it into the blood of a goat they had killed. Then they took the coat and returned home to Jacob. They said to their father,

"This is what we have found. Was it not Joseph's robe?" Jacob recognised it and said, "It is my son's robe. A wild beast has devoured him. Joseph has been torn to pieces." (Genesis 37: 31–33)

Poor Jacob mourned because he believed his son was dead but fortunately before the story ends Joseph and his father were reunited finally.

Prayers

1   Dear Father God, thank you for our clothes. Thank you for warm garments to wear in the winter when it is cold and for cool clothes in the summer. Thank you for our school uniforms, our best clothes and for clothes in which we can go out to play. Thank you for special clothes for the beach and for holidays and for clothes we change into when we go to bed at night. Help us to look after our belongings to show that we are grateful for all that we have. Amen.

2   We thank you, God, for our mothers who knit and sew for us, for people who work in factories cutting out clothes, machining, weaving and sewing; we thank you for all those whose work brings the materials to the factories. Please bless all who work to keep us clothed. Amen.

3   Lord Jesus we like to have nice clothes and look smart, but help us, too, to think about all the poor people who have so much less than we have. Amen.

Hymns

Thank you Lord for this new day (CP 32)
When I needed a neighbour (CP 65)

~ ~ ~ ~ ~ ~ ~ ~ ~ ~ ~ ~ ~

G is for George

George and the dragon

St George is the patron saint of England and his special day is 23 April. George was not an English man but he was adopted by the English people as their saint because he encouraged the knights in their crusades.

George lived about two hundred years after Jesus and

he became a soldier in the Roman army. When he became a Christian he left the army, because one of the things the soldiers had to do was to seek out Christians and put them in prison.

Many legends are told about St George, but the best known is the one about George and the dragon. When George was on one of his expeditions he came to a city where everybody was living in fear. This was because a fierce and terrible dragon had come to live in the lake close to the city. Whenever the dragon felt hungry it roared into the town, devouring anything it could find to eat. The people were terrified and stayed indoors to avoid the terrible beast. But towards evening they would begin to hear the roaring and see the smoke and the flames coming from its mouth as the dragon approached the city again.

For a long time the people managed to hold the dragon off, by leaving food for it outside the town. But the dragon was a big creature with an enormous appetite and before long it had eaten not only all the food but every wild and tame animal that the people sacrificed for it. The monster demanded to be fed or it would charge into the city and burn down the houses of the people and devour them. The king of the land did not know how to keep peace among his people. The only answer he could think of was for one person to be offered to the dragon each day. The people agreed to draw lots to see who was to be the first person to be given to the dragon for his supper. So this went on each day, and nobody knew until the day began whether or not they would be killed and given to the fiendish dragon before the day was over. Each day brought fresh fear for the people who were still alive in that city.

Then came the fateful day when the king's daughter was the one whose name was drawn for the evening sacrifice. The king was full of grief but the girl was very brave and she went forward to meet her death with courage. She went down to the water's edge and waited for the dragon to appear. But the sound which she heard did not come from the dragon. It sounded more like the galloping of a horse. Riding towards her came a knight in shining armour. St George rode in to attack the dragon and a terrible fight took place. The dragon was strong and powerful, but again and again St George charged at the monster, until at last with his sword he gave him a fatal wound and the dragon lay dead at his feet. St George then took the princess back to her father.

The king promised St George any reward he wanted. But George said his victory was won through God's strength alone. He wished for no reward, other than to see the people of the kingdom acknowledge Jesus as their Lord, so that they would all become Christians. So the people praised God who had sent St George to them at a time of great trouble. George had proved himself to be a man of great strength, courage and faith and because of all these qualities he was chosen by the people of England to be their saint. Let us try to follow in the footsteps of St George and never to lack the courage to do what we know is right.

Prayers

1 Teach us, good Lord, to serve you as you deserve,
  To give and not to count the cost,
  To fight and not to heed the wounds,
  To toil and not to seek for rest,
  To labour and not to ask for any reward,
  Save that of knowing that we do your will. Amen.

2 St George he was a goodly knight,
  Renowned for all his wondrous might,
  For every deed he said the same,
  "I do this, in God's Holy Name." Amen.

3 O Lord our Heavenly Father, keep alive in our hearts the spirit of adventure, that we may be like St George in the stories of old. Make us scorn the way of safety and help us to obey your will. Help us to be worthy of those brave people who in every age have been prepared to give themselves in obedience to your call, through Jesus Christ our Lord. Amen.

Hymns

Soldiers of Christ arise (WCV 52)
When a knight won his spurs (WCV 66)

~ ~ ~ ~ ~ ~ ~ ~ ~ ~ ~ ~

G is for Goliath
David and Goliath

The story of David and Goliath is a very well known story in the Old Testament. (1 Samuel: 17) It tells how David the shepherd boy fearlessly faced the fiercest soldier in the army of the Philistines. He turned what would have been a terrible defeat into a great victory for King Saul and his army.

A war was being fought between the Israelites and the Philistines. King Saul was king of the Israelite people and he had strong armies which he led into battle. Three of David's older brothers were in the army, but David was still too young to be a soldier. His work was with the sheep, minding the flocks for his father who was becoming old and weak.

The battle was not going well for the Israelites. All their forces were gathered on one hill, and the army of the Philistines was camped opposite. Among the men in the Philistine army was a man named Goliath. He was their champion. He was a man of great height and strength. He was very fierce and frightening. He wore heavy armour to protect himself. He had heavy weapons and he always sent his shield-bearer marching ahead of him. Every morning and evening Goliath used to come out and shout across to the Israelites, "Why do you come out to do battle, you slaves of Saul? I am the Philistine champion; choose your man to meet me. If he can kill me in a fair fight we will become your slaves, but if I prove too strong for him and kill him you shall be our slaves and serve us."

There was not one soldier in Saul's army who felt able to meet the challenge of this champion, Goliath. Each man was afraid to be the one to face the giant. And so for forty days Goliath offered to fight and with each day that passed the Israelites felt more and more ashamed.

David's father asked David to go and visit the camp of the soldiers, taking some food for his brothers, and to bring back a token to show that all was well. David was pleased to obey his father. He left early in the morning and reached the Israelites' camp just when the soliders were taking up their positions. He ran to talk to his brothers, getting news of them to take back to his father. Then Goliath came out and shouted his challenge. David was shocked at the rude way Goliath called out to his people and he asked his brothers, "Who is this man who dares to defy the army of the living God?" David's brothers were impatient with him. They treated him as a young boy and told him to go back to his sheep. So David tried to find out more about Goliath from some of the other men.

Word reached King Saul that David was saying he was prepared to fight Goliath. Saul sent for David and David said to him, "Do not lose heart, sir. I will go and fight this Philistine." But the king replied, "You cannot go and fight with this Philistine. You are only a lad and he has been a fighting man all his life." But then David explained to Saul that he was a shepherd boy, and shepherds faced all kinds of dangers every day. David said he had already slain a lion and a bear which had attacked his father's sheep. He said to Saul, "This Philistine will fare no better than they. He has defied the army of the living God. The Lord who saved me from the lion and the bear will save me from this Philistine."

So Saul agreed that David should go out and fight Goliath. He was very anxious that David should borrow his armour and wear it. He put his tunic on David and placed a bronze helmet on his head. He fastened a sword to the tunic and gave David a coat of mail to wear. But David felt strange and uncomfortable in all this armour. He said, "I cannot go with these because I am not used to them." Instead he went to meet Goliath wearing the clothes of a shepherd boy and carrying his sling, the only weapon which he knew how to use. He also carried five smooth stones for the sling which he had chosen from the brook. Fearlessly he stepped forward to face the giant, Goliath, a man nearly three metres tall.

When Goliath saw David coming to do battle with him, he was angry. He thought the Israelites were mocking him by sending a mere boy to fight against him. He roared at David, "Am I a dog that you come out against me with sticks? Come on and I will give your flesh to the birds and the beasts." David answered bravely, "You have come against me with sword and spear and dagger, but I have come against you in the name of the Lord of Hosts, the God of the army of Israel which you have defied. The Lord will put you into my power this day."

Goliath moved forward, ready to attack David, but before he could take his spear, David took a stone from his bag and used his sling to send it spinning through the air. The stone hit Goliath on his forehead, a spot where he was not protected by armour, and he fell to the ground. And so the victory was David's. The Lord had watched over him as David's faith had proved and there was great rejoicing among the Israelites who then defeated the army of the Philistines. King Saul was very pleased with David and kept him at his court.

Prayers

1   Dear Lord, may we be like your servant David, fearless in times of danger and prepared to fight for what is good in your name, knowing that you will be with us at all times. Amen.

2   When in danger make me brave,
    Make me know that you can save,
    And when all alone I stand,
    Shield me, with your mighty hand. Amen.

3   Give us faith, Lord, to know that your arm is there to protect us and your spirit to guide us as we go through life. When we meet difficulties upon the way, make us brave and fearless. Give us the courage of David to stand up for you when others would deny you. Make us strong soldiers in the army of the living God. Amen.

Hymns

Come my brothers, praise the Lord (CP 20)
He who would valiant be (WCV 40)

~ ~ ~ ~ ~ ~ ~ ~ ~ ~ ~ ~

H is for Hands
Jesus' hands

Let us think for a moment about all the things we have used our hands for today. There were many occasions when Jesus used his hands. His hands blessed the little children, took the loaves and the fishes and blessed the food before it was given to the people, and touched the deaf, the blind and the lame as he healed them. His hands washed the feet of the disciples, and broke the bread at the Last Supper. His hands, scarred with the wounds of the nails, helped Thomas to believe the wonderful truth that Christ had risen from the dead. His hands were the hands of a carpenter, skilled in a particular craft. His hands showed us the sort of person he was. Take a look at your hands. Are you always going to feel proud of them?

There are many stories told about different people, who had reason to be proud of the work of their hands.

Kitty Wilkinson

One person whose hands were gnarled and arthritic through hard work was a woman called Kitty Wilkinson. She lived in Liverpool many years ago when there was a terrible outbreak of cholera. Many people in Liverpool died and many of those who were not ill moved away from the city to places where they would be safe. Kitty did not catch cholera, but she didn't run away either. She stayed in Liverpool and she gathered together all the children who had lost both their parents in the sickness. She took in forty-five orphans and she spent the rest of her life working to support them. She scrubbed floors, took in washing, did anything that would bring in more money to feed and clothe her children. She didn't feel heroic at the time, but she felt a very real love and concern for those who needed her. Her life's work is still remembered by the people of Liverpool.

The man with the withered arm

There was a man once who came to Jesus. It was in the synagogue on the Sabbath Day. This man had a withered arm, an arm he could not use, so he was unable to work and he was very poor. He had to beg for the little money he needed to buy food. His life was miserable because he knew his arm would never get better. The people who had gathered in the synagogue wondered what Jesus would do about this man. They knew that Jesus would touch and heal all those who came to him. But on the Sabbath Day people were not allowed to do any work. It was a day that had to be kept holy. There were some among the crowd who would have liked to accuse Jesus of doing the wrong thing. Jesus knew what they were thinking when they said to him, "Is it permitted to heal on the Sabbath?" (Matthew 19: 9–14) Jesus answered them by saying, "It is permitted to do good on the Sabbath," and he told the man who was waiting to be healed to stretch out his arm. "He stretched it out and it was made sound like the other." It must have been a wonderful moment for him when he felt the power and strength of God's healing moving through his arm and into his hand so that he could begin to live a normal life.

Prayers

1 Thank you, dear God, for our hands and what we can do with them. Help us always to use them to be kind and helpful. Amen.

2 Jesus' hands were used a lot,
To help and heal and show the way;
They had great strength,
They had great warmth,
They worked hard every day.
May my hands be strong hands, too,
And may they loving be,
That every day someone may say
They see God's love in me. Amen.

3 O God, who has commanded that no one should be idle, give us grace to use all our skills and talents in your service and for the service of others; that whatsoever our hands find to do, we may do it with all our might. Amen.

Hymns

Hands of Jesus take the bread (SM 42)
He's got the whole world in his hand (CP 19)

~ ~ ~ ~ ~ ~ ~ ~ ~ ~ ~ ~

H is for Happiness
Two boys in hospital

We like to feel happy and we are lucky because we have been given enough good gifts to make us full of happiness each day. We can show our gratitude for all that we have by being cheerful, happy, joyful people. When you meet someone who has a happy, smiling face and who doesn't keep on grumbling about things that go wrong, it makes your own heart feel light and gay. Happiness is infectious. It spreads from one person to another. Let us make sure that someone catches a little happiness from us each day. A famous poet once wrote these words, "Life is so full of a number of things. I'm sure we should all be as happy as kings." If we decide we are going to be happy people we can certainly find plenty of things which we can be happy about. We will find, too, that we have lots of friends, because people will enjoy our company if we are always cheerful.

There is a story told about two little boys in hospital. Both had been in the same ward for a long time and both were going to have to spend a few more weeks together in the hospital. The boys were about the same age. They had had similar operations. They had about the same number of visitors each day. You would have thought that both boys would have had the same things to be pleased about and the same things to grumble about. But the boys were very different. One was very sorry for himself. He was miserable every day because he couldn't get up. He thought about his friends at school and decided it wasn't fair that he had to spend all his days in bed in a hospital ward. He often grumbled and felt unhappy. The other little boy had a very cheerful nature. He would tell jokes and smile at the nurses. He was always glad to see visitors and talked to them cheerfully, listening happily to the stories they told him. He was glad that although he was in hospital the doctors were doing their best to make him well again.

As the two boys lay in bed each day, the happy one had his bed near to the window. He told his friend about all the things he could see from his window to try to cheer him up. He described the people who passed by and all that they were doing. He talked about the trees and flowers he could see growing and the cats and dogs in the garden below. All the time he chatted, he made the scene outside the hospital window sound exciting and interesting. His friend used to listen to all the tales and he felt rather jealous that he couldn't see out. It gave him another reason to grumble, instead of being grateful that his happy companion in the ward shared all his fun with him.

One day the happy little boy was taken out of the ward. He had to have another operation on his leg, but he left cheerfully, sure he would soon be back feeling better. When the other boy was left alone he really did miss his friend. He asked the nurse if his bed could be moved over to the window so that he would be able to look at all that was happening outside. The nurse was surprised but she agreed to move his bed across. You can imagine how surprised the boy was to discover that there was no view from the window at all. All he could see was a grey brick wall and on the ground beneath were two dustbins. Then the little boy realised what his friend had been doing for him. He had been making up exciting stories to keep him cheerful and happy, although there had been no difference at all between them. He felt a little ashamed of his past selfishness and decided that, like his friend, from that moment on, he would try and spread a little happiness to someone else.

Prayers

1 Thank you for each happy day,
   For fun, for friends, for work and play,
   Thank you for your loving care,
   Here at school and everywhere. Amen.

2 O God, it is easy to be happy when we are enjoying ourselves and all is going well. Help us, we pray, to keep smiling and cheerful in the face of difficulties. Give us the will to spread a little happiness each day. We ask this in your name. Amen.

3 O Father of goodness
   We thank you each one
   For happiness, healthiness,
   Friendship and fun,
   For good things we think of

And good things we do,
And all that is beautiful,
Loving and true. Amen.

4   Give me a good digestion, Lord,
And also something to digest.
Give me a healthy body, Lord,
With sense to keep it at its best.
Give me a healthy mind, good Lord,
To keep the good and pure in sight,
Which seeing sin is not appalled,
But finds a way to set it right.

Give me a mind that is not bored,
That does not whisper, whine or sigh;
Don't let me worry overmuch
About that fussy thing called I.
Give me a sense of humour, Lord,
Give me the grace to see a joke,
To get some happiness from life,
And pass it on to other folk. Amen.

Hymns

I saw raindrops on my window (SM 60)
Join with us to sing God's praises (CP 30)

~ ~ ~ ~ ~ ~ ~ ~ ~ ~ ~ ~ ~

H is for Harvest

The harvest festival

Harvest is a time of thanksgiving. It is a time when every
one likes to thank God for all his good gifts. Thanksgiving
for harvest is a very old custom and so the harvest hymns
and songs are mostly about the crops and the fruits that
provided the main store of food for the winter.

Modern farmers have machines, but they still plough
their land, sow their seed and harvest the crops. They still
depend on the sun and the rain and the wind to grow and
ripen their crops. So our harvest celebrations may have
changed a little but the meaning of the harvest festival is
still the same. God has provided for all our needs, and so
let us say thank-you for offering back to God some of the
wonderful gifts he has supplied to us.

The rice harvest in Japan

A farmer in Japan worked extremely hard because he badly needed the income from his harvest of rice. It was the time of harvest thanksgiving and the rice that he had sown and planted had been gathered in and was ready to be threshed. All the people of the village were crowded together by the seashore, where the celebrations were taking place. The farmer was still high up in his farmland home looking down on the scene below. He noticed a strange light in the sky and he could see a great wave gathering far out to sea. He felt the ground tremble beneath his feet. He knew the village would soon be rocked by a great earthquake, and the sea would break over the shore.

The farmer knew he must save the people who had gathered down there. He had to do something drastic to get them away from the coast and higher up the hillside to safety. Suddenly an idea came to him. He fetched a light and began to set fire to each of his stacks of rice until they were all burning fiercely. The people down by the coast saw the smoke in the sky and saw the flames leaping up from the land owned by the farmer. They realised that a fire had broken out on his land and they hurried towards his home to see what help they could offer.

As they climbed the mountain the great waves crashed on the beach behind them. The farmer lost all his harvest of rice, but he had offered it as a way of saving the lives of the people in his village. It was an unselfish act of great sacrifice. He had given all of his harvest for a greater good.

Prayers

1 O God you are Lord of the Harvest,
   The giver who gladdens our days,
   Our hearts are for ever repeating
   Thanksgiving and honour and praise. Amen.

2 O Lord our Heavenly Father we thank you for all your gifts at harvest time. For the corn and fruit of the field and orchard, for the harvest of the sea and for all useful things from the mines beneath the earth. May we, who have plenty, remember those in need and may we never waste your gifts but use them and share

them for the sake of him who lived and died for us, Jesus Christ our Lord. Amen.

3   God has filled the mountains with metals hard and
      bright;
    Man has learned to mine them and bring them to the
      light;
    Man has made them into tools, great machines and
      cranes,
    But who made man? Why, God made man, and God
      gave man his brains.

    God has filled with wonders the earth on which we
      dwell;
    Man has learnt their powers and usefulness to tell:
    Man has made his telephones, cars and aeroplanes –
    But who made man? Why, God made man, and God
      gave man his brains.

    So let us praise the Father for mines beneath the rocks,
    The whirring power-stations, the steamships and the
      docks,
    The magic of the radio, the thunder of the trains,
    For man made these, but God made man, and God
      gave man his brains.

Hymns

We plough the fields (WCV 86)
The earth is yours, O God (CP 6)

~ ~ ~ ~ ~ ~ ~ ~ ~ ~ ~ ~ ~

H is for Homes

Our homes

At the end of each day we look forward to going home. We enjoy being with our families, sharing with our brothers and sisters, telling our parents about the events of the day, sometimes asking for their help or showing them new skills we have learned. Our families make home the place where we most like to be. We need to feel the love and care of our families and we have to give them our love too.

When we think of our homes and families and all that home means to us, it might make us think about people who are in special 'homes' and why they are there. There are special homes for the blind, for handicapped people, for the elderly, for the mentally ill, and for children who have no parents. All these special homes are run by people who spend their time looking after others. They love and care for the people in the homes as if they all belong to the same family.

Dr Barnado

Many special homes which look after people were started a long time ago, when there was a lot of poverty. There were many people who had to sleep on the streets at night. There were people with no shoes who were dressed in rags and had no warm clothing for the cold weather. There were people who died of cold and starvation without anyone to care for them.

One person who helped change these things in London was Dr Barnardo. When Barnardo first came to London he had no idea how his life was going to change. He came to train as a doctor because he wanted to be a missionary and to work in China. He was a very active Christian. He went to Church every Sunday and while he was a student in London he went to poor areas to teach the people about Jesus. Often Barnardo was attacked, but he had a forgiving nature, and little by little the people came to trust him. When he discovered how many poor children there were in London, with no schools to go to, he opened a school for them. His school was held on Sundays and in the evenings. He realised that he had a lot of work to do for God in London so he gave up the idea of going to China and spent more and more time teaching in the areas around London.

One night when his school closed he discovered that some of the boys had nowhere to spend the night. When he tried to send them home they said they had nowhere to go and no-one to care for them. Barnardo could hardly believe this was true, but the boys took him out into the streets and showed him where little children were sleeping together in the open, huddled up to keep warm. He knew he had to do something about this terrible state of affairs. He prayed to God for an answer to this problem. At last he decided to open a home for children.

At first Barnardo only accepted as many children as he could afford to look after. One night he turned away a boy because he had no room for him. Although Barnardo had given this boy money to buy food the boy died that night of cold and starvation. From that moment on Barnardo said he would never turn away any child who came to him in need of care. Over the door of his homes he put up a big notice which said, "No destitute boy or girl ever refused admission." When he died there were thousands of children who were grateful for his life's work. Somebody said of Barnardo, "Earth is poorer now but heaven is richer." That is a wonderful thing to be said of someone who always listened to the voice of God directing him. Dr Barnardo's homes still look after children in need.

Let us be truly thankful for our own homes and let us remember all the people who work in homes for people in special need.

Prayers

1   God of all our cities,
    Each alley, street and square,
    Pray look down on every home
    And bless the people there. Amen.

2   Lord Jesus, friend of little children, we thank you for those who have served you in their life time and those who are serving you now. We pray for those who work in homes, taking care of the old, the sick, the handicapped and the homeless children. May we also be kind to all who need our love and may we make our own homes happy places. Amen.

3   May the love of God our Father
    Be in all our homes today,
    May the love of the Lord Jesus
    Keep our hearts and minds always,
    May his loving Holy Spirit
    Guide and bless the ones we love,
    Fathers, mothers, brothers, sisters,
    Keep them safely in his love. Amen.

Hymns

Lord of all hopefulness (100 HT 61)
O God in heaven whose loving plan (100 HT 74)

~ ~ ~ ~ ~ ~ ~ ~ ~ ~ ~

H is for Hope
The boy who fell overboard

I am sure you know what it is to hope. Perhaps you hope it will soon be playtime, or maybe you hope there will be sausages for dinner! "Don't give up hope," we say, and people rarely do. The sorrowing disciples were filled with hope when they discovered the empty tomb on Easter Sunday morning. Jesus Christ was alive. Their worst fears were over. Hope has kept many people alive when they have been faced with great danger. Many people who have been rescued from dangerous situations have said that they never once gave up hope.

A young boy once left school and joined the navy. The young sailor had not been long on his first ship when he was ordered early one morning to scrub the decks. He began to work but unfortunately he slipped and fell overboard into the sea. He could not swim well and no one on the ship had seen him fall. The sailor called out loudly but the ship sailed on and no one heard his desperate cries for help. As he watched the ship disappear he fought for his life.

An hour later at breakfast, there was an empty place where the young sailor usually sat and his shipmates began to ask where he was. With alarm, they realised that the boy had been missing since he had been on deck. They told the captain at once and he told everyone exactly what to do. The time and the distance that the ship had travelled were carefully calculated and the captain set a return course to take them back to where the sailor had disappeared. Everyone knew that the chances of finding the boy were very small. The hearts of the men were heavy as they watched the waters, watching for a sign of life. They had lost hope. But suddenly the captain ordered that a boat should be lowered. The impossible had happened. He had spotted a head bobbing up and down on the waves. The young sailor was rescued after two and a half hours alone in the water. The captain later went to see him as he lay in bed recovering. "What kept you alive?", asked the captain. "You must have lost all hope of being found." "Oh, no, sir," said the sailor, "I never lost hope. I know you, and I knew that you would come for me."

That story tells us a lot about the courage of the young sailor and also about the concern of the captain for his men.

Prayers

1   O Lord Jesus Christ, who rose from the dead, to bring hope and to comfort your disciples, grant that we may follow your example and make a point of encouraging people when they are in difficulties or in need. May our presence bring to others the same hope and comfort that your presence brings to us each day. Amen.

2   O Father of goodness,
We thank you each one
For happiness, healthiness
Friendship and fun,
For good things we hope for
And good things we do,
And all that is beautiful
Loving and true. Amen.

3   Lord Jesus Christ we bring before you all that we hope for this day. Hear our prayers and help us to please you in all that we do as we go about our work and play. Amen.

Hymns

Lord of all hopefulness (WCV 45)
Through the night of doubt and sorrow (WCV 53)

~ ~ ~ ~ ~ ~ ~ ~ ~ ~ ~ ~

I is for Ignorance

Sita's Christmas preparations

Sometimes you may hear people saying, "Ignorance is bliss." It is something people say if they hear something they don't like the sound of. But God has given us minds to think with and we know that we are meant to use all our gifts and talents to the full. So we should try not to remain ignorant.

There is a story about a small village in India where the people had not heard about Jesus. Some years ago, a woman called Sita moved from a large town in India into a much smaller village. As Christmas approached she began to make all the usual preparations; she cooked, made decorations, packed presents for her family and began to feel excited as the day got nearer. Sita did not know many people in the village, and so she did not notice straight away that nothing much was happening in preparation for Christmas. But gradually she realised that no one but her own family was making any preparation.

The people in the village did not know about Christmas. They had never heard of Jesus. They could not celebrate what they did not know or understand, so Christmas for them was not going to happen. Sita felt sad. She had so looked forward to this happy time but she and her family would be the only people in the village keeping the birthday of Jesus. She knew it was the sort of occasion that has to be shared by everyone in order to be truly happy. Sita decided she must do something about it. She went to the shops and bought as many ingredients as she could afford and then when she got back home she started to cook. She made lots and lots of sweets, which she wrapped up into little parcels. When she was sure she had enough, on Christmas Eve she went to every home in the village and left a packet of sweets as a present for each child. Everyone was surprised to see Sita. They did not know why she was giving presents to everybody but they thought it was very kind of her.

The following day, which was Christmas Day, the mothers sent all their children round to Sita's house to say thank you for the sweets she had brought for them the night before. The children were a little shy at first, but they knocked at Sita's door and said, "Thank you" as they had been told. Then one little boy, who was a bit bolder than the others, asked "But why did you make sweets for us all?" Then Sita sat down with the group of children gathered around her, and she began to tell them about the baby born in the stable at Bethlehem. She told them about Mary and Joseph and the angels, the shepherds and the kings, the story of the first Christmas, which we know so well, but these little children were hearing for the very first time.

And what joy they felt in that village as they celebrated the birthday of Jesus and how gladly the children came back to Sita again and again after that day to hear more about Jesus. They were no longer ignorant about the love of Jesus, which they could all share.

Prayers

1   O God, our Heavenly Father, we are glad of all the opportunities for learning that we have at school and at home. As we enjoy our work each day, help us to grow in knowledge and to share what we learn with others. Amen.

2   O Lord, we pray for all people who work in other lands, bringing the good news of Jesus to those who have not heard of you. Please bless them and protect them from danger and help them in their difficulties. Through Jesus Christ our Lord. Amen.

3   Dear Jesus we pray to you to send among us the true understanding of life, so that we shall not remain ignorant of all your good gifts. Teach us to be ready to work and ready to play, ready for serious thought and ready for fun, so that we may grow up following the example which you have set for us. Amen.

Hymns

The ink is black, the page is white (SM 10)
He gave me eyes (GP 18)

~ ~ ~ ~ ~ ~ ~ ~ ~ ~ ~ ~

I is for Innocence

Jesus' trial

When you have had an accident in the playground and you are asked what happened, very often you say, "It wasn't my fault." You are telling me that you are innocent. We always want to make sure we are not blamed for something we have not done. We want everyone to know that we are innocent so that we do not get into trouble. If you are always truthful people will believe you when you say you are innocent. But it is very wrong to pretend you are innocent if you are not. This can lead to someone else being punished for something you did.

Sometimes, it happens that we have to take the blame for something that really wasn't our fault. Jesus taught us that when this happens we have to try and forgive those who have made a mistake and judged us wrongly. Jesus was sometimes blamed for things he had not done. Towards the end of his life, his enemies told a lot of lies about him because they wanted to see him punished and put to death. When he was being tried he was brought to the court of Pontius Pilate. Pilate's wife sent a message to Pilate when Jesus was standing before him as a prisoner. She warned Pilate, saying, "Have nothing to do with that innocent man. I was much troubled on his account in a dream last night." (Matthew 27: 19) But Pilate did not listen to his wife's warning and he allowed his soldiers to take Jesus away. He was not happy about his decision, though, and he said to the people who were shouting to have Jesus crucified, "I am innocent of this man's death. It is your decision and your responsibility."

Pilate was wrong. He knew that Jesus had never committed any crime, and he should not have allowed him to die. He could only pretend he was innocent of Jesus' death. He had allowed his soldiers to take Jesus away to be crucified.

Holy Innocents' Day

A few days after Christmas, on 28 December is a special day called "The Holy Innocents". On this day we remember all the baby boys who died in Bethlehem and the surrounding district after Mary and Joseph had escaped with Jesus to Egypt. King Herod had asked the three wise men to come and tell him when they found the new born king. He pretended that he wanted to worship him, but really he wanted to harm the baby, so that his position as king would not be threatened. When time passed and the wise men did not return Herod became furious. He gave orders that all the children aged two or less were to be killed. He felt sure then that the child whom the wise men had worshipped would be put to death. The mothers of the children who died grieved for their babies. The children were too little to have ever done anything wrong. They were innocent. Therefore the day is called Holy Innocents' Day. Let us try each day ourselves to remain innocent of any wrong action.

Prayers

1 Dear Heavenly Father, we are thinking of Jesus, who gave his life that we might live, even though he was innocent of any wrong doing. Fill our hearts with wonder and gladness for the great victory which has been won for us. Amen.

2 Heavenly Father, whose children suffered at the hands of Herod, though they did no wrong, give us grace neither to act cruelly, nor to stand indifferently by, but to defend the weak from the tyranny of the strong, in the name of Jesus Christ who suffered for us, but is alive and reigns with you and the Holy Spirit, one God, now and for ever. Amen.

3 We are new born Christians
We must learn to fight
With the bad within us
And to do the right.

Christ is our own Master
He is good and true
And his little children
Must be holy too. Amen.

Hymns

It fell upon a summer's day (WCV 63)
Saviour teach me day by day (WCV 60)

~ ~ ~ ~ ~ ~ ~ ~ ~ ~ ~ ~

I is for Invitations
The invitation to the feast

I am sure you all like to receive invitations. You have probably had invitations to go and play with your friends, invitations to go out to tea or invitations to a birthday party. On such occasions you must remember to behave well and to thank the people who have asked you to their home. I expect there have been times when you have invited someone to your house to play. When you invite people home you have to look after them and allow them to share your things and make them feel happy to be with you. So whether you receive or give an invitation, there are certain things you have to remember to do.

Jesus told a parable about invitations. (Luke 14: 15–24) One day a man decided to give a special dinner party. He invited all his best friends to the party. He went to a lot of trouble to arrange a really good dinner and he thought carefully about what his guests would like to eat. Then he sent out his servant with a message to tell the guests that he was ready to receive them. The servant called on all the people who were invited to say his master was waiting for them. It was time for the party to begin. The man was very upset as one guest after another started to make excuses not to come to the party. One of his friends wasn't coming because he had bought some new land and had to stay and look after it. Another had said he had changed his mind because he had five oxen which he wanted to put to work. Another said he was staying at home because he had just got married. When the man heard that no one was coming to his party he was upset and angry. He was determined that some one should enjoy all the food. So he sent his servant out again.

This time the servant was told to go round the streets and alleys and find all the poor people, the blind, the crippled and the lame and to bring them back to the house. The servant did this and he came back to his master again and said, "Sir, your orders have been carried out and there is still room." So his master replied, "Go out again and wherever you meet anyone who will come to my party, invite him here, for I want my house to be full." And so those people who came to the dinner party were ones who had not been invited in the first place.

75

Jesus loves and offers hospitality to us all. In his kingdom there is room for everyone. He said that it is sometimes kind to invite somebody who can't invite you back.

Prayers

1   Lord Jesus we thank you that you have invited us all to share in your kingdom. We want to come to you. We want to learn to love you as you love us. Please help us to grow more like you each day. Amen.

2   Thank you God for friends.
Thank you for fun and games and parties.
Thank you for best friends and friends to share things with.
Help us to be friendly to those we do not like as much and make us willing to include them in our invitations. Amen.

3   Praise God for lovely surprises,
He fills us with laughter and fun,
When he asks us all to his party
He knows we'll be glad to come. Amen.

Hymns

Lord of all hopefulness, Lord of all joy (WCV 45)
Lord Jesus Christ, you have come to us (100 HT 58)

~ ~ ~ ~ ~ ~ ~ ~ ~ ~ ~ ~

I is for Isaac

The birth of Isaac

Abraham believed and trusted in God. He listened to God's voice and obeyed him. God was very pleased with Abraham and he led him to a new land where he could settle and make his home. Abraham's wife was called Sarah, and God promised Abraham that one day she would have a son. Abraham did not believe this could happen because he and Sarah had been married a long time. They were both getting old and still they had not had any children. But God spoke to Abraham and said, "I will bless Sarah and give you a son by her. I will bless her and she shall be the mother of nations; the kings of many

76

people shall descend from her. You shall call your son Isaac." (Genesis 17: 16–20)

About a year later a baby boy was born to Sarah. Abraham and Sarah called their son Isaac and they were both full of joy. Sarah was so happy she said, "God has given me good reason to laugh, and everybody who hears will laugh with me." And so Isaac grew up in a home where his parents loved him very dearly. (Genesis 21: 6–7)

God knew that Abraham was a good man and so he chose him to be the father of his people.

Isaac is offered as a sacrifice

God wanted to be sure Abraham would always remain true to him and that he would trust in God no matter what terrible things might happen. One day God decided to test Abraham to make sure he was as strong a man as God believed him to be. (Genesis 22: 1–14)

God spoke to Abraham. He told Abraham he was to take his only son Isaac, whom he loved dearly, and go on a short journey. When they reached the place God had chosen, Abraham was to offer Isaac as a sacrifice to God. Abraham did as God had commanded him. He prepared for his journey and took two of his servants with him. He took wood to light the fire for the sacrifice, he saddled his donkey. He called Isaac early in the morning and they and the two servants set off for the place that God had chosen. The journey took three days. When they were near the place, Abraham told the two servants to wait while he and Isaac went on alone to worship God. Abraham gave Isaac the wood to carry, and Isaac felt sure something strange was going to happen. He said to Abraham, "Father, we have the wood for the fire, but where's the young animal for the sacrifice?" Abraham was full of sorrow but he replied, "God will provide for the sacrifice, my son."

When they reached the spot, Abraham built an altar and placed the wood on it. Then he took his beloved son, Isaac, and placed him on top of the altar. Just as Abraham was preparing to offer the sacrifice, the Lord called to him from Heaven, "Abraham, Abraham." Abraham answered, "Here am I." And then an angel spoke to him and said, "Don't raise your hand against the boy. Do not touch him. You are a man full of faith. You have proved your trust in

God and would have offered even your son, your own son." Then as Abraham looked around him in wonder, he saw a ram caught in the bushes. This was the sacrifice that God had provided, and joyfully Abraham and Isaac worshipped together. God spoke to Abraham again and said to him, "Because you have done this and have not withheld your only son, I will bless you abundantly. All nations on earth shall pray to be blessed as you are blessed and this is because you have obeyed me."

So Isaac too grew up putting all his trust in God and later he married Rebecca and they were very happy.

Prayers

1   O Lord God, who chose Abraham to be the father of your people, give us such faith that we may trust in you always, never doubting your love and care for us. Amen.

2   Father God, we ask you to bless all families and to fill the homes where children are growing up with love, laughter and happiness. Amen.

3   May this day be full of power that shall bring us nearer to you, Lord Jesus, and make us more like you. May we so trust you this day, that when the day is over, our trust shall be firmer than ever. Amen.

Hymns

Blest are the pure in heart (WCV 44)
Praise my soul the king of heaven (WCV 18)

~ ~ ~ ~ ~ ~ ~ ~ ~ ~ ~ ~ ~

J is for Jacob

Jacob and Joseph are reunited

Jacob was Joseph's father. He had not seen his favourite son, Joseph, since the day he had sent him out to visit his brothers who were caring for the sheep. They had taken away Joseph's special coat and sold him to some merchants. They told their father that Joseph must have been killed by a wild animal. Jacob thought this was true and he grieved for Joseph very much.

Many years passed and there was a famine in Egypt and other lands. Jacob heard that there was corn in Egypt, so he told ten of his sons to go there and buy some. He kept his youngest son, Benjamin, at home with him, so that no harm should come to him. (Genesis 42: 1–4)

The ten brothers reached Egypt and they were taken to the governor who sold the corn. The governor was Joseph, but his brothers did not recognise him. He pretended to be very harsh. He demanded to know where they came from and why they had come. The brothers explained, but Joseph pretended not to believe them and said they must be spies. He said he would only believe they were telling the truth if they went back to Canaan and returned with their youngest brother. The brothers went back to Jacob and told him how harsh the Egyptian Governor had been to them. He did not want to let Benjamin go with them but they became so short of food that Jacob had to agree. He said to them, "Take your brother with you and go straight back to the man. May God almighty make him kindly disposed towards you." (Genesis 43: 13–14)

So all Joseph's brothers came again to Egypt and Joseph was full of joy when he saw that they had returned with Benjamin. Still the brothers did not know that it was Joseph. He prepared a feast for them all and the brothers presented gifts which Jacob had told them to take to the governor. Joseph asked some anxious questions. He asked them how they all were and said, "Is your father well, the old man of whom you spoke? Is he still alive?" they answered, "Yes, my Lord. Our father is still alive and well." (Genesis 43: 27–28) Joseph looked hard at Benjamin and asked, "Is this your youngest brother of whom you told me?" Joseph was overcome by his feelings and close to tears.

When they had finished eating and driinking, Joseph told his attendant to fill the sacks of the visitors with grain and he told him to put a silver goblet in the top of Benjamin's sack. Next day the brothers departed, but before they had gone far Joseph sent his steward after them to search the sacks of grain. The silver goblet was discovered in Benjamin's sack and all of them had to return. Joseph pretended to be very angry but said they could all go free, except the one whose sack had contained the goblet. That brother, he said, must remain in Egypt and become his servant. The brothers did not know what to do. They had promised their father that they would protect Benjamin. They knew they could not return without him. One of the brothers, Judah, pleaded with Joseph to let him remain in Egypt instead of Benjamin. He explained to Joseph that it would break Jacob's heart if Benjamin did not return home safely.

Joseph could not keep up his pretence any longer. He sent away all his attendants and stayed in the room alone with his brothers. Then he said to his brothers, "Come closer. I am your brother Joseph whom you sold into Egypt, but don't be alarmed. It was God who sent me ahead of you to save men's lives. Make haste and go back to my father and give him this message from his son Joseph. "God has made me Lord of all Egypt. Come down to me. Do not delay. I will take care of you and your household and all that you have. There are still five years of famine to come." Then Joseph kissed all his brothers and forgave them.

When Jacob heard that Joseph was alive, he could hardly believe it. He was very old but he was determined to go and see Joseph before he died. God spoke to Jacob and told him not to be afraid to go to Egypt and so he set off with all his household. Joseph told Pharaoh that his father and brothers had come to him and wished to settle in Egypt and Pharaoh said they should have some of the best land. Joseph brought his father and presented him to Pharaoh and then Joseph cared for him and his brothers in their new home.

Prayers

1   Dear Lord Jesus, we thank you for our families, for our mothers and fathers, our brothers and sisters. Help us to show our love by obeying our parents and by forgiving each other, just as Joseph was ready to forgive his brothers. We ask this in your name. Amen.

2   Help us, O Lord, to think about all the members of our family and to care for each of them. May we remember the special needs of those who are very old and may we be protective and loving to those who are younger than ourselves. Amen.

3   Father God we thank you that we are growing up in homes which are full of love, surrounded by the care of our parents and families. Help us to bring joy into our homes so that we make them happy places we will remember with love as long as we live. Amen.

Hymns

Fill your hearts with joy and gladness (CP 9)
O God, thou art the father (WCV 122)

~ ~ ~ ~ ~ ~ ~ ~ ~ ~ ~ ~ ~

J is for Jairus

Jairus' daughter is cured by Jesus

Jairus was an important man. He was president of one of the synagogues. He was known and respected by all the people of the town. Jairus was a rich man and he lived in a fine house. He had servants to wait on him. He had a wife and a little daughter about twelve years old, whom he loved very dearly. Jairus must have been very happy with his life and contented with his home and his work.

One day his daughter became desperately ill. She seemed to be dying, for she was getting weaker all the time. Jairus knew of Jesus and he felt certain that Jesus would be willing to come to his house and could make the little girl well again. So he left his house and went down to the shore. (Mark 5: 21) A great crowd was gathering round the lake, for word had spread that Jesus was returning. Jairus made his way through the crowd until he came close to Jesus and then he threw himself down at Jesus' feet and begged him for help. He said, "My little daughter is dying. I beg you to come and lay your hands on her to cure her and save her life." (Mark 5: 23)

Jesus left at once to go to the house, accompanied by Jairus and a great crowd of people. The crowd kept jostling against Jesus and Jairus, as they hurried through the streets. Among the crowd was a woman who had been ill for a very long time. She, too, desperately wanted to reach Jesus. She felt sure that if she could just get near enough to touch his robe, then her sickness would leave her. Eventually she managed to stretch out her hand and just touch the gown Jesus was wearing. Her sick body immediately felt strengthened but Jesus stopped. He had felt a special power going out from him and he knew that someone in distress had come to him for healing. Jesus turned to the people in the crowd and said, "Who touched my clothes?" His disciples said to him, "You see the crowds pressing upon you and yet you ask, 'Who touched me?'" (Mark 5: 31) They thought Jesus had just felt people pushing against him and did not realise Jesus had stopped for a special reason. The woman understood what was happening, but she felt afraid. Perhaps Jesus would be angry that she had pushed herself forward and dared to touch him. She came and knelt in front of Jesus and told him the whole truth. Jesus understood. He spoke kindly to the woman, saying, "My daughter, your faith has cured you. Go in peace, free for ever from this trouble."

This delayed their journey to the president's home. A messenger came running to find them. He sought out Jairus and said to him, "Your daughter is dead. Why trouble Jesus any more?" Jesus overheard what was said, and he turned to Jairus and comforted him, saying, "Do not be afraid. Only have faith." He then told the crowd they were to come no further and he went on with Jairus, accompanied only by Peter, James and John.

As they got close to the house they could hear people crying and wailing as they mourned for the little girl. Jesus went up to them saying, "Why this crying and commotion? The child is not dead. She is asleep." They did not believe Jesus. They laughed at what he said, mocking him. But again Jesus turned all the people away. He went into the house with only the child's parents and his three chosen companions. Jairus and his wife took Jesus to the room where their daughter was lying. He went across to the little girl, took hold of her hand and said to her, "Get up, my child." Immediately she got up and began to walk about. Jairus and his wife and the three disciples were filled with wonder.

Prayers

1   Lord Jesus give us faith to trust in you completely. When we turn to you for help, make us understand that you are always there. Make us ready to ask, believing that you will always do what is best for us. Amen.

2   Loving Father, we ask you to bless all those who are ill and in pain. Help them to feel that you are their father, and that your love is all around them. Amen.

3   Lord how glad we are that we don't hold you, but that you hold us. Amen.

Hymns

I danced in the morning (CP 22)
Jesus shall reign where'er the sun (WCV 67)

~ ~ ~ ~ ~ ~ ~ ~ ~ ~ ~ ~ ~

J is for Jonah

Jonah and the great fish

Jonah was one of the prophets of God who we can read about in the Old Testament. One day God spoke to Jonah and told him to go to the city of Nineveh. The people there had been behaving badly and God was going to punish them and destroy their city. God told Jonah to go there and warn the people. Jonah did not like the idea. The people of Nineveh might even kill him, he thought, if he told them all the terrible things God had warned him were going to happen. So he decided to run away and hide. He went as far away as possible from Nineveh and hid on a ship that was about to sail for Spain.

Jonah must have thought that his plan was working. But no one can hide from God. A terrible storm began to gather. The sailors on the ship were scared. They thought the ship was going to sink and that they would all be drowned. They gathered together and prayed to their own gods to save them. Still the storm raged on, and then one of the sailors discovered Jonah and shouted out to him. (Jonah 1: 6) "What, sound asleep? Get up and call on your God. Perhaps he will spare us a thought and we shall not perish." Then Jonah realised that he was the cause of all the trouble on board the ship.

The sailors threw overboard all the things they could spare to lighten their load, but this did not help. Next they cast lots to find out who was bringing them so much bad luck, and Jonah's name was drawn. They said to him, "What is your business? Where do you come from? What is your country? Of what nation are you?" (Jonah 1: 8) And Jonah answered, "I am a Hebrew, and I worship the Lord of heaven, who made both sea and land." The storm by this time was getting even worse and Jonah knew he must act. He said to the sailors, "Take me and throw me overboard and the sea will go down. I know it is my fault that this great storm has struck you." (Jonah 1: 12) So they took Jonah and threw him overboard and the sea stopped raging.

Then the Lord sent a great fish which swallowed Jonah. He remained inside this fish for three days and three nights. During that time Jonah prayed to God, begging forgiveness for what he had done wrong. Then at the end of the three days, the Lord spoke to the fish and it spat Jonah out on to the dry land. (Jonah 2: 10)

God spoke again to Jonah and told him he must go to the city of Nineveh and carry out the task of warning the people about their wicked ways. This time Jonah obeyed. After three days' journey, Jonah made his proclamation to the people. He cried out to them, "In forty days Nineveh shall be overthrown." (Jonah 35) The people of Nineveh were very much afraid. They knew that Jonah was a prophet sent to them by God. They realised the wrong that they had done and they were deeply sorry. They began to fast and they dressed themselves in sackcloth, to show everyone that they really meant to do better. Even the king rose from his throne. He dressed himself in sackcloth and he said they would turn back to God and show how sorry they were. God forgave them. He did not send the disaster he had threatened.

But Jonah was very unhappy about this. He felt that

God should have punished the people of Nineveh. He told God that the people would mock him because he had warned them of a punishment they did not receive. Jonah did not want God to forgive the people, even though they had shown they were sorry and were trying to be better.

Jonah left the city and sat down on the ground. It was very hot with no shade, and so God made a plant grow up over Jonah to give him some shade. Jonah was grateful but the next day God sent a worm to attack the plant, and it withered and died. A scorching wind began to blow and the hot sun beat down on Jonah's head. He felt very ill. God said to Jonah, "Are you angry? Are you sorry that the plant had to die?" (Jonah 49) Jonah said he felt very angry. Then God said to Jonah. "You are sorry about the plant, which you did not have the trouble of growing. It came in the night and died the next day. Do you not think that I am sorry for the great city of Nineveh and the one hundred and twenty thousand people who live there? Do you think I want to see all that go to waste?"

Then Jonah understood. Jonah blessed the city of Nineveh, and thanked God for the mercy he had shown.

Prayers

1   Lord God our Father, you have promised to forgive us when we have done wrong and we are truly sorry for our sins. Forgive us this day any wrong that we do and help us, in our turn, to be forgiving to others. Amen.

2   Dear Jesus, there are times when we are afraid, when we do not want to do the things we have to. Help us at such times to act courageously, knowing that you are with us and will care for us. Amen.

3   Almighty God, watch over us all today. Forgive us our faults, forget our mistakes, and give us time and opportunity to learn to be good examples of Christian life, through Jesus Christ our Lord. Amen.

Hymns

God is working his purpose out (WCV 72)
Father hear the prayer we offer (WCV 26)

~ ~ ~ ~ ~ ~ ~ ~ ~ ~ ~ ~ ~

J is for Joseph

Joseph becomes ruler in Egypt

After Joseph had been sold to some merchants by his brothers, he was taken away to the land of Egypt. There he was sold as a servant and he had to work for Potiphar, a captain of the guard. Joseph was a loyal servant and a hard worker. Potiphar began to depend on Joseph more and more. (Genesis 39: 4) He thought highly of him and gave him many rewards. Potiphar's wife, though, became jealous of Joseph. She told lies about him and betrayed him, and so Joseph was sent to prison.

Two other servants shared his prison cell. One was Pharaoh's butler and the other his baker. Both these men kept having strange dreams. Joseph told the butler and the baker what their dreams meant. He said the butler was going to be set free but the baker would be hanged. All this actually happened, but Joseph himself still remained a prisoner. And then Pharaoh began to be troubled by dreams. He had a vision of seven fat cows and seven thin cows. All the cows would go down to the river to graze. Then the seven thin cows began to devour the seven fat cows and at this point Pharaoh would wake up. (Genesis 41: 4–5) When he fell asleep again, he dreamt another strange dream. he saw seven full ripe ears of corn growing on one stalk, and then seven thin ears followed and they swallowed up the good corn. Pharaoh could not understand these strange dreams and he badly wanted someone to explain them to him. The butler told Pharaoh about Joseph, so he commanded that Joseph be brought to him.

Joseph came to Pharaoh and he told him that his dreams had only one meaning. God was warning him that there would be seven years of good harvests, but these would be followed by seven years of famine. Joseph said that Pharaoh needed to appoint a firm ruler, who would build great store houses and save food during the plentiful years. Then when the famine reached the land, the people would be able to use the food they had carefully stored away.

Pharaoh decided that all Joseph said was true and he said there could be no better man than Joseph to be in charge of the preparations. So Joseph became ruler in Egypt, second only to Pharaoh.

As God had foretold in Pharaoh's dreams, the next seven years were years of plenty with abundant harvests. Joseph stored the grain in huge quantities. Then the seven good years came to an end and the seven years of famine began. There was a famine in every country, but in Egypt there was bread. More and more people appealed to Pharaoh for food and he, in turn, sent them to Joseph. Joseph opened all his granaries and he sold corn to the starving people. (Genesis 41: 57)

Everyone wanted to be in favour with Joseph now because he could save them from starvation. Joseph had started his life in Egypt as a slave, but because of his truthfulness at all times, his loyalty to his master and his trust in God, he was finally in a powerful position. There must have been times though when he thought about his father and wondered about his brothers and the home he had left. Joseph could not have realised that his careful plans for the future would lead his family back to him.

Prayers

1 Grant, O Father, that we may always act wisely and truthfully. Give us a clear vision about which path we should take and help us to remain true to it, whatever the difficulties. Amen.

2 Dear Lord Jesus, we thank you that each year you provide for our harvests that we may always have enough to eat. We pray for people in other lands where food is scarce and where men, women and children go hungry and starve. Help us to find ways of helping them. Amen.

3 O Lord God, King of the universe, blessed are you, who brings forth bread from the earth. Amen.

Hymns

O praise him, O praise him (CP 13)
God is working his purpose out (WCV 72)

~ ~ ~ ~ ~ ~ ~ ~ ~ ~ ~ ~

J is for Justice
Dick Whittington

Dick Whittington came to London because he had heard that its streets were paved with gold. Dick was so poor and life was so hard that he nearly gave up the struggle to make a living. However, in time Dick Whittington became Lord Mayor and this story reminds us that he was just, honest and kind in everything he did.

A young sailor called Jack was going home to London to visit his mother, who was a widow. Even though his wages were small, he had saved a little money to help her. On the way home, he sat on a bench and saw a little bag on the ground. In it were twenty golden coins. Jack was an honest boy so he took the bag to the town crier and told him how he had found it. "You are in luck," said the town crier. "I have just announced the loss of the gold. If you return it to the merchant at the inn, he has promised a rich reward." Jack was well pleased and he hurried to the inn.

The merchant was delighted when he saw the bag in Jack's hand. But he was a greedy, dishonest man and did not want to part with the reward he had promised. He pretended to Jack that the bag had contained a precious emerald as well as the twenty golden coins and he accused Jack of stealing the jewel.

Jack knew the merchant was lying and he was determined that justice should be done. He insisted on going to the Lord Mayor's Court to have their case heard.

The Lord Mayor was none other than Dick Whittington himself. He listened carefully to the story which Jack told. Then it was the merchant's turn to tell Dick Whittington how he had been robbed of the emerald.

Dick listened patiently to both. He saw that Jack had an honest face. He noticed, too, the greedy look in the eyes of the merchant. Dick Whittington was sure which man was speaking the truth. "The bag that you found," he said to Jack, "you say contained nothing other than twenty golden pieces." "Yes, sir," replied Jack. Dick Whittington then turned to the merchant, "The bag you lost," he said, "you say contained twenty pieces and a precious emerald." "That is so," replied the merchant. "Well," said Dick Whittington to the merchant, "I am convinced that the bag in front of me has not been tampered with in any way. I am certain this bag never held a jewel and so it cannot be the bag you lost. I therefore hand this bag and its contents over to Jack and hope, sir, that you will find your lost property very soon."

Dick Whittington left the court. He had seen that Jack was justly treated for his honesty. The merchant, too, maybe learnt a lesson. If we wish for justice for ourselves, we must act with equal justice towards each other.

Prayers

1 O God, help us to be just and fair in all our dealings. We ask this in the name of your son, Jesus Christ our Lord. Amen.

2 Almighty God, by whom we are taught that all men are equal in your sight; help us to fight injustice wherever we may find it and to live in peace with our neighbours, for Jesus Christ's sake. Amen.

3 O God, our judge of all that is true, make us strong and courageous so that we may ever stand firmly and uphold what is right and live in your love. Amen.

Hymns

O God thou art the Father (WCV 122)
If I had a hammer (SM 11)

~ ~ ~ ~ ~ ~ ~ ~ ~ ~ ~ ~

K is for Kennedy

The life of J. F. Kennedy

John Fitzgerald Kennedy was President of the United States of America. There were nine children in the Kennedy family and they were brought up in a Christian home as members of the Roman Catholic Church. John's father used to say to his children that he did not mind what they chose to be when they grew up, so long as they did their job well. "Even if you're going to be a ditch-digger," he said "be the best ditch-digger in the world." John never forgot what his father told them as children.

When John Kennedy was a young man his country was at war, and he was in the American Navy. One dark night, Kennedy's ship was hit by the enemy and it started to sink. Two members of the crew died and one sailor was badly injured. Kennedy encouraged all the others to swim to the part of the ship that was still above the water while he went to rescue the one who was injured.

The next day Kennedy persuaded all his men to swim to a deserted island, as the rest of the ship was sinking. Kennedy towed the injured sailor to the shore. All of them reached the island, but there was no water and very little food. That day they ate snails and drank coconut milk but this made them sick. So on the next day, even though he was very tired. Kennedy swam to another island, looking for food and water. When he reached a third island he found a little canoe, a container of water and a tin of biscuits. He loaded up the canoe and set off back to his companions. But a storm blew up and Kennedy nearly drowned. He was saved by some natives from a small island, but they could not speak English. With his knife he scratched a message onto a coconut shell. He tried to explain to the natives that they should contact the American base so that a rescue party could be sent. Eventually news spread that some Americans had been shipwrecked and a boat was sent to pick up the sailors, who had been kept alive by Kennedy's determination and brave spirit. Kennedy refused to take any leave when he got home. He immediately joined his next ship, although he was suffering from a bad back injury.

Kennedy was the youngest person ever to be elected president of the United States and people wondered what sort of president he would be. Kennedy was a very strong and determined person. He saw a lot going on in his country that he disagreed with and he began to change things. One of the things Kennedy wanted, was for all people to be treated equally, whether they were black or white. He knew it was right that every person should have the same opportunities in life. But there were people who did not agree with Kennedy, so he made enemies as well as friends.

One sad day when John Kennedy was visiting the town of Dallas, in Texas, he was shot dead whilst driving in an open car. The gun had been fired by a man who thought he could get his own way by using violence. Kennedy is remembered as a man who served his country in war and peace without fear or thought for himself. He made the very best of the job he had chosen for life, as his father had told him to do when he was still a small boy.

Prayers

1   Lord Jesus, you, too, knew what it was like to have enemies as well as friends. You were brave when you were betrayed and when you suffered on the cross. We, too, would be brave when we try to do right. Make our lives good lives, so that whatever we choose to do, we may do it to the best of our ability. Amen.

2   Father God, we pray for the men and women who lead their countries and who have to make difficult decisions. We pray for our Queen and for the Prime Minister and leaders all over the world. Please help them to act wisely and for the good of others. Amen.

3   God, our Father, creator of the world, please help us to love one another. Make nations friendly with other nations, make all of us love one another like brothers. Help us to do our part to bring peace in the world and happiness to all men. Amen.

Hymns

Rejoice, O land, in God thy might (WCV 22)
I will bring to you (CP 59)

~ ~ ~ ~ ~ ~ ~ ~ ~ ~ ~ ~ ~

K is for Kindle
The legend of Prometheus

To kindle something means to set fire to it. If you light a bonfire, a camp fire or a fire in a hearth, you have to look after the first flames carefully so that the fire will kindle and not go out. We also speak of the Holy Spirit kindling a flame of love within our hearts. We want this fire to burn brightly. Fire is a powerful force. It can be very dangerous, but it is a great gift if it is used wisely.

Prometheus was a Titan and most of the Titans had been imprisoned underground by Zeus, the chief of the gods. The Titans were a gigantic race. They were also strong and Zeus was afraid they might become too powerful. But Prometheus had been useful to Zeus in the past, so as a reward he remained free. Prometheus lived with men on the earth and he saw how weak they were. They seemed unable to compete with the strength and ferocity of the animals and unable to protect themselves. Prometheus decided that men needed to have fire as a weapon and an ally. Fire had never been heard of on earth. It would have to be stolen from the sun. But Zeus guarded the mountain above which the sun blazed.

Prometheus was very daring. He climbed Mount Olympus and he plucked from the sun's rays a red flower of fire. He fixed the flower to a reed and brought it back to earth. Then Prometheus gave his prize as a gift to men. After that, men discovered they could do all kinds of wonderful things, unknown to them before. They could make strong weapons, dig iron from the ground, drive away wild animals and keep themselves warm. The men began to get much stronger and more powerful. But Zeus had been watching all that was going on. He was very angry. He did not want men to become so powerful. He realised that men were using fire to help them get control over the earth and he knew that only Prometheus could have got the fire for them.

Prometheus had to be punished. Zeus had him bound in chains and tied to a rock. All day the sun beat down on Prometheus. The only relief he had was when night came. For a long time Prometheus had to suffer for the gift he brought to the human race, but eventually Zeus relented, and Prometheus was free again.

Prayers

1 O Lord, kindle in the hearts of all men a love of peace.
Keep alight within us the flame of your spirit that we
may please you in all that we do. Amen.

2 We thank you, O God, for all your gifts to us. Today
we thank you especially for the gift of fire and for the
many uses we can make of it. Help us to use all your
gifts in the way that you intend. Amen.

3 Kindle in us, O God our Father
The power of the Holy Spirit to strengthen us,
The guidance of the Holy Spirit through our con-
science,
The inspiration of the Holy Spirit so that we may know
your will,
Through Jesus Christ our Lord. Amen.

Hymns

Colours of day dawn into the mind (CP 55)
All creatures of our God and King (WCV 8)

~ ~ ~ ~ ~ ~ ~ ~ ~ ~ ~ ~ ~

K is for King
The legend of King Canute

The king of a country is a very important person. The
people of his kingdom honour, obey and serve him. He, in
his turn, has to be a good servant to his people and try to
help them and govern in the best possible way. Prince
Charles will be our king one day. His motto, as the Prince
of Wales, is "I serve". Whenever you see pictures of Prince
Charles on the television you see him meeting and talking
to the people, encouraging them and trying to understand
their difficulties and problems. He has done a lot to help
young people and handicapped people. His grandfather,
King George VI was a very good king, too. He ruled over
us during the last war and he helped many people who
had lost their homes and their loved ones. Some people
called him "George, the dutiful" because he always put his
duty to God and his people before thinking of himself.

A thousand years ago King Canute ruled England. He
was a good king and much loved by his people. But some

of his courtiers would praise the king in a very exaggerated way. The king was quite a humble man so he thought all this praise was silly. The courtiers were saying that there had never been another man as great as the king, and that nothing was impossible for him. So one day King Canute decided to teach them a lesson.

Canute ordered his servants to carry his royal chair down to the seashore and told his courtiers to follow him. When the chair was put into position at the water's edge, the king sat on it. Very soon the tide began to turn and the sea lapped nearer and nearer to the royal throne. The king held up his hand, raised his voice and called out, "Sea, come no nearer. You shall not wet the feet of this great king." But the tide still came closer to the royal chair. Very soon the waves were breaking against Canute's feet. With each wave, the king spoke again, telling the sea to go back. The courtiers looked on with amazement as the king continued to order the sea back. Then Canute got up from his throne and came up the beach to them. He said, "Now you have seen for yourselves that for me there are many tasks that are not possible. I spoke to the sea and it did not obey me. There is only one whose voice can calm the storm and the winds. He is the Lord our God, who rules heaven and earth. He is the God whom you should worship. Keep your praise and give the glory to Him."

The courtiers knew that King Canute was right. They felt ashamed of their silly ways and there, on the seashore, they knelt down and asked God to forgive them and help them to act more wisely.

Prayers

1   Almighty God, Lord of life, help us to remember that you have made all things, and that all things belong to you. Be our guide day by day and when we do things well, may we always be thankful to you. Amen.

2   Jesus, our King, you reign for ever over us. Yet you are also our friend, our helper and our guide. May we praise you and serve you all our lives and through our service may we help each other. Amen.

3   Yours, Lord, is the greatness, the power, the glory, the splendour and the majesty; for everything in heaven

and earth is yours. All things came from you, and of your own do we give you. Amen.

Hymns

All nations of the earth (CP 14)
We have a gospel to proclaim (100 HT 98)

~ ~ ~ ~ ~ ~ ~ ~ ~ ~ ~ ~ ~

K is for Knowledge

The boy Jesus in the temple

The word "knowledge" does not sound as if it begins with the letter "k" but you can think of other words like "knife" and "knee" that have a silent "k" at the beginning. The more knowledge we have, the wiser we become. The wiser we become, the more we can succeed in the things we most want to do and the more we shall be able to help and serve others.

When Jesus was a boy, children did not have the same opportunities to go to school and learn as you do. The girls were expected to help their mothers. They had to learn to cook and help to carry water, and shop at the market. The boys were taught to read and write by the rulers of the synagogue so that they would be able to read the scriptures. The boys would learn their letters by drawing them in the sand.

Jesus was very keen to learn all that he could. He concentrated hard on his reading and writing and he tried to understand all he could about God. Jesus and the other boys in Nazareth looked forward to the day when they would go with their parents to Jerusalem, the city of the big temple. Many people travelled there each year to keep the feast of the Passover. The journey from Nazareth to Jerusalem was a long one by foot. Donkeys would be loaded up to carry some of the things necessary for the journey.

When Jesus was twelve, preparations were made to go to Jerusalem for the Passover, and he was included. When they reached Jerusalem, Jesus was filled with wonder at the sight of the temple. He could not spend enough time there. The family stayed in Jerusalem for the week of the festival and every day there were special services to attend. Jesus was greatly interested in everything that happened. He went to the temple whenever he could and listened attentively to the priests.

The week passed very quickly, and Mary and Joseph were planning the return journey. On the last day shortly before they were going to leave, Jesus slipped away again to the temple for one last visit. There were many people with Mary and Joseph, so they left without noticing that Jesus was not with them. Jesus did not realise how quickly the time was passing. He was listening to the teachers, asking questions and answering them when he could. He was not thinking about anything else.

By the end of the day, the travellers grew tired and stopped for a rest. Mary and Joseph looked round for Jesus but could not see him. They asked their friends but no one could remember seeing Jesus. Mary and Joseph felt very anxious as they returned to Jerusalem. By the time they had got back, three days had passed. When they looked in the temple they found Jesus among the teachers, joining in with them as they talked together. Everyone was amazed by the knowledge and intelligence of a boy of only twelve.

Mary had been so worried that when she saw Jesus she said to him, "My son, why have you treated us like this? Your father and I have been searching for you." (Luke 2: 48) Jesus was surprised to find her so upset and he replied, "What made you search? Did you not know that I was bound to be in my Father's house?" Mary and Joseph did not fully understand what Jesus meant but Mary never forgot the words which he spoke to her that day.

Prayers

1 O Lord bless our school, that working together and playing together, we may learn to serve you and to serve one another. Amen.

2 Father of us all, help us to have another happy day at school. Help us to learn new lessons, gain new know-ledge and play new games with our friends. Help us to make the most of all the opportunities you give to us each day. Amen.

3 Our Father, will you near us stay,
When we sleep and work and play,

Will you guide us every day?
Hear us, Heavenly Father. Amen.

4   Grant to us, O Lord, to know what is worth knowing,
    to love what is worth loving, and to hate all that is evil
    in your sight. Amen.

Hymns

Lord and saviour true and kind (WCV 34)
The wise may bring their learning (CP 64)

~ ~ ~ ~ ~ ~ ~ ~ ~ ~ ~ ~ ~

L is for Lent

Jesus in the wilderness

Lent is a special time in the Christian year when we prepare for the great festival of Easter. It is a time when we think about ourselves and try to examine ourselves. We find out what is bad about us, like getting angry or being selfish, and try to be better. At the same time we look for our good points, and try to polish them up. We also think about other people, especially people who are not so fortunate as ourselves, and we see what we can do to help.

Lent begins on Ash Wednesday and lasts for forty days and forty nights, the same length of time that Jesus was in the wilderness. Jesus went into the wilderness after he had been baptised by John in the River Jordan. He wanted to be on his own, so that he could prepare himself quietly for the great work he was about to begin. He was ready to leave his home and go out among the people, teaching and healing them, and helping them to realise that the kingdom of heaven was a kingdom of love, open to everybody. Jesus knew he would face many difficulties, and his time in the wilderness was spent in prayer to God, seeking strength and guidance from his Father for all he was going to do.

Ash Wednesday

At Easter we welcome the spring, and during Lent the days begin to get lighter and longer. That is the meaning of Lent. It means lengthening, and we watch the days drawing out and enjoy the longer evenings. The name "Ash Wednesday", the first day of Lent, comes from long ago, when people used to dress themselves in sackcloth at the beginning of Lent and put ashes on their heads. This was to show that they were sorry for their past misdeeds and were going to make an extra effort to do better. In some churches people are still marked with the sign of the cross in ashes on their foreheads on the first day of Lent. It is a mark of being sorry. It was also a sign that people would try to fast, to go without some food during Lent, remembering that Jesus was hungry in the wilderness, just as many people are hungry in the world today.

We should try all through the year to grow more like Jesus, but Lent gives us a chance to start again if, from time to time, we forget our good intentions.

Prayers

1   O God our Father we thank you for the forty days of Lent. We want to be more like you. Help us always to act unselfishly and to care for the needs of others. We ask this for Jesus' sake. Amen.

2   O God, who loves a cheerful giver, help us to find happiness in the things that we can do for each other. May we always remember to give a helping hand to those in need and teach us that the joy of giving is the real joy of living. Amen.

3   Lord Jesus Christ, we confess to you now the wrong things we have done, the wrong things we have said, the wrong in our hearts. Please forgive us and help us to live as you want us to. Amen.

Hymns

New every morning is the love (WCV 2)
Gentle Christ, wise and good (SM 12)

~ ~ ~ ~ ~ ~ ~ ~ ~ ~ ~ ~ ~

L is for Lepers

Father Damien

When Jesus sent his twelve chosen apostles out into the world, he said to them "Heal the sick, raise the dead, cleanse lepers, cast out devils." (Matthew 10: 8)

In those days there was no cure for leprosy, and people who became ill with it eventually died. Leprosy usually started by the sick person's hands or feet becoming numb and then often they became infected because there was no feeling left. Large sores would develop on the person's legs, arms, bodies and face. Everyone was terrified of catching the disease. If someone became a leper, he became an outcast. He would have to leave his home and his family and live on his own, or with other lepers, because nobody else wanted to come near him. He had to keep away from the town and hope that food would be left where he could collect it when there was nobody about. It was a very lonely life for a sick man with nobody to care about him.

Leprosy continued to be a dreaded illness until quite recently. Medical science has now brought about cures which make the illness much less serious than it used to be, and far fewer people catch it. But for a long time after Jesus had gone back to his father in heaven, men and women who became lepers continued to be isolated and cast out from their homes.

There was a famous man called Father Damien, who was a Roman Catholic priest and a missionary. His dedication and service to a community of lepers who had been abandoned on an island helped all people with leprosy. Father Damien volunteered to be the priest for all the sick people on the island. He knew that in the end, he would surely catch the illness himself. For sixteen years he worked as a priest, a teacher, a builder and a friend for the lepers. Those who were less ill helped him with his work. He built a new church, a new school and new homes for people to live in. He also found a source of fresh water, so that the lepers could wash and cook and drink. This had been impossible for them until Father Damien came.

There was nothing Father Damien would not do for those lepers. He loved them, he nursed them, he comforted them. Although the work that he did was endless, he began every day with prayers, which he said in his church. More and more of those island people came back into God's family through Father Damien. It was a sad day when he himself became a leper. He had always been a happy and a cheerful man and he did not let his illness change him. He said he was glad that God had chosen him to be a leper like the people he served, and thanked God that he had been chosen to be the priest for that island.

When Father Damien died, a wonderful thing happened. All the terrible sores and the signs of illness that had spread over his face completely disappeared. God had worked another miracle through the life of Father Damien.

Prayers

1 We bring to you, O God, in prayer, all missionaries who have left their homes to go to distant lands.

protect them in all their dangers and help them with all their difficulties, so that they may never be lonely or afraid, because you are with them. For Jesus Christ's sake. Amen.

2   Our Father God, we know that your son Jesus Christ went about doing good and healing all kinds of sickness among the people. Help us to be kind like him and to remember those who are ill today. Send down your blessing on all doctors and nurses who work to prevent suffering and so follow the loving kindness of our Lord Jesus Christ. Amen.

3   For all the strength we have,
    Our thanks to you we pray,
    May we be quick to help the sick,
    Today and every day. Amen.

Hymns

Go tell it on the mountain (CP 24)
Join with us to sing God's praises (CP 30)

~ ~ ~ ~ ~ ~ ~ ~ ~ ~ ~ ~ ~

L is for Likeness

The blind men and the elephant

People sometimes say, "What is God like?" The answer is that we don't know exactly. We have some very good ideas about what God is like because his son, Jesus Christ, came to show us. We are told that we are made in the likeness of God, but the picture we have of Him is not likely to be the whole one. It is rather like the answers given by the blind men who were asked to describe an elephant.

An Indian prince gathered together in the market place all the blind men who lived in the town. Near them he placed an elephant. Then he told each man in turn to touch the elephant and describe it. The first man came. He placed his hands on the head of the elephant and felt it. "The elephant", he said, "is like a pot."

Then the next blind man had a turn. He happened to catch hold of the elephant's ear. After feeling it carefully he announced, "The elephant is like a fan."

The third blind man grasped the tusk. It was firm and

101

hard, smooth and shiny to the touch. "Why", he said, "the elephant is like the handle of a plough."

But the fourth blind man was feeling the trunk. He laughed. "The elephant is just like a snake," he said. The fifth blind man, who was feeling the elephant's broad back said clearly, "The elephant must be like a barn."

Then the sixth blind man took hold of a leg. "This elephant", he declared, "is just like a pillar." The seventh blind man approached from behind. He took the elephant's tail into his hand. "The elephant is like a rope," he announced.

But yet another blind man was feeling the tuft at the end of the elephant's tail and he declared, "The elephant is like a feather duster."

The prince listened to all these descriptions. Not one of the blind men had any idea what the gigantic animal before them was like. Each had been right in one small detail but not one of them could imagine the greatness of the elephant and the wonder of the whole creature.

Prayers

1   Lord God, you have made us in your own likeness. Help us to grow more like you each day. Amen.

2   Dear Jesus, open our eyes to see what is beautiful, our minds to know what is true, our hearts to love what is good, that we may be like you, our Lord and master. Amen.

3   Day by day, dear Lord, of thee
    Three things I pray,
    To see thee more clearly
    To love thee more dearly
    To follow thee more nearly
    Day by day. Amen.

Hymns

Jesus Lord we look to thee (WCV 62)
Jesus humble was your birth (100 HT 46)

~ ~ ~ ~ ~ ~ ~ ~ ~ ~ ~ ~

L is for Luke

Luke the writer

St Luke's special day is 18 October. St Luke lived at the time of Jesus and was a close friend. He saw all the good that Jesus did as he went round healing and helping. He listened to the lessons Jesus taught and heard the parables he told. Luke wrote down the events he could remember in the Gospel according to St Luke.

Some of the stories of Jesus are in all the gospels, each told a little differently, depending on the writer. But in each of the gospels we can also find stories not told in the other three gospels, which perhaps the other three writers had forgotten. For example, it is only in the Gospel of St Luke that we find the story about Jesus healing the lepers, of whom only one came back to say thank you. Another story found only in the Gospel of St Luke is the parable of the Good Samaritan. We would have lost a lot if St Luke had not written these stories down for us.

It was also Luke who wrote the Acts of the Apostles. In this book we learn about what happened as the apostles set out to carry on God's work when Jesus went back to his Father in heaven.

Luke the doctor

Besides being a very fine writer, Luke was a doctor. He did not have all the equipment, medicines or knowledge that doctors have today, but he must have been a man of great compassion with a desire to care for others. Luke loved Jesus and served him all his life. Because he was a medical man, Luke was chosen to be the patron saint of doctors and on his feast day, 18 October, we always remember those people who are ill and the doctors and nurses who care for them.

Prayers

1   Almighty God, who inspired Luke the physician to proclaim the love and healing power of your son; give your church, by the grace of the spirit, and through the medicine of the gospel, the same love and power to heal, through Jesus Christ our Lord. Amen.

2 Great Father in Heaven, thank you for doctors and nurses everywhere. Thank you for their skill in making sick people well. Please bless them in all their work. Amen.

3 O Lord Jesus Christ, you healed the sick and helped all those who came to you in need. We ask you to give to all doctors and nurses, skill, gentleness and patience. Bless all those who suffer and help them to find rest and comfort, healing and peace of mind. We ask this, in your name. Amen.

Hymns

At the name of Jesus (SM 39)
Would you walk by on the other side (CP 70)

~ ~ ~ ~ ~ ~ ~ ~ ~ ~ ~ ~

M is for Mercy
Dionysius, Pythias and Damon

Many years ago rulers had great power and some of them used their power badly. They were cruel to the poor, unjust in giving punishments and they often had no mercy. But sometimes cruel rulers change their ways through the example of others. This happened in Greece, to the ruler, Dionysius over two thousand years ago.

Dionysius was a hard and cruel man. He thought he was very important but he cared little about hardship and suffering of others. One day, two friends called Pythias and Damon were walking in the streets of the town. Pythias was talking to Damon about Dionysius' cruelty. Unfortunately the conversation was overheard by a soldier who pounced on the two friends and dragged them away to the court. They were brought before the ruler and because Pythias could not deny what he had said about Dionysius, he was condemned to death. Both the friends were heartbroken when they heard this sentence passed. Pythias, who was to die, asked for one merciful act from his ruler. He begged Dionysius to allow him to travel home to say goodbye to his mother before he died. Dionysius laughed him to scourn, "Do you think I don't know that you would escape and go into hiding?" he said.

But Damon was a true friend. "I will take the place of Pythias in prison," he told Dionysius. "Pythias is a loyal man. He will return before the time of his execution in four weeks. If he does not come back, then I will die in his place."

Dionysius was surprised by the trust and the courage of Damon and he agreed to let Pythias go on his last journey. Damon remained in prison. The first week passed. Then the second and the third. Finally the last week approached. Each day went by with no sign of Pythias.

The day of the execution arrived and Dionysius came to Damon. "Your friend has let you down," he said. "Now you must die in his place." "Pythias will still come if he is alive," Damon answered. But the soldiers were already dragging him away.

Suddenly a great shout went up among the crowd. Pythias was running towards Damon. "My friend," he gasped, "I'm just in time. My boat was shipwrecked and I have been delayed for days, but at least I am here now." The friends greeted each other warmly. Dionysius was amazed by such loyalty. Even his cold heart began to melt and he dealt mercifully towards the two men. "You shall both go free," he declared, "for two friends who can be so loyal towards each other do not deserve to die."

Dionysius felt a much better person for having shown mercy and from that day onwards he became a wiser and fairer ruler.

Prayers

1   Our Father in Heaven, please have mercy upon us for the wrong things we have done. For bad temper and angry words, for being greedy and wanting the best for ourselves, for making other people unhappy. Dear Jesus, please forgive us. Amen.

2   Lord Jesus we remember how you showed mercy upon those people who hurt you. Help us to forgive those who hurt us. May we never try to pay them back. Amen.

3   May grace, mercy and peace from the Father, the Son and the Holy Spirit, be with us all this day and always. Amen.

Hymns

All people that on earth do dwell (WCV 10)
Praise to the Lord, the Almighty, the King of creation (WCV 17)

~ ~ ~ ~ ~ ~ ~ ~ ~ ~ ~ ~ ~

M is for Missionaries

David Livingstone

One of the last commands that Jesus gave his disciples was that they should go out into all the world to teach people of every nation and baptise them. These apostles were the first missionaries of the church. They left their homes and went to strange places where they knew nobody, and they worked hard to spread the teachings of Jesus. Ever since that time there have been men and women who have wanted to serve Christ in this special way. They have wanted to devote the whole of their lives to working in a particular place where they know the native people are in need of help.

David Livingstone was born in Scotland. His parents were poor people, so he had to leave school when he was only ten years old and go to work. After a long day at the factory, David would get hold of all the books he could and study late into the night. David was sure that God had chosen him for some special mission. He knew that he would not spend all his life in the factory so he used every chance he had to learn. It must have been very hard for him and sometimes he must have been very tired but he never lost sight of his ambition.

David felt that God was calling him to go to China and so he went to London to prepare for his journey. But war broke out in China and no one was allowed to leave for that country, so David was delayed in London. He trained as a doctor, believing it would be useful for him to heal as well as to teach the people he was going to convert to Christianity. In London, David Livingstone met a man who had been working as a missionary in Africa. He listened to tales about this little-known dark continent and he knew that he must go there.

So David Livingstone, the missionary doctor, set out on his life's work. He moved round many of the African villages and his care of the sick helped him to win the confidence of the native people. They trusted Livingstone and they listened to his teaching of the gospel. Many African people became Christians. Some of Livingstone's first African friends offered to make more of the Africans into Christians by beating them and making them listen. They found it hard to understand how Livingstone wanted them to live peacefully together as Jesus had taught. As the Christians grew in number they realised that Livingstone's peaceful methods really worked. More and more African people were prepared to help by work-ing at the mission stations which he set up in some of the villages. Here he taught the people and cared for all the sick.

One of the things which disturbed David Livingstone very much was the slave trade. From time to time hordes of savages would attack a village and capture men and women. They would then take them in chains to white settlements. From here they were sent away and sold as slaves, never to see their own homes or families again. Once, he came across some newly captured slaves waiting to be transported from their village. He released them from their chains and handcuffs and set them free. In this way he made enemies of the people who were making money by selling slaves. He worked tirelessly to bring the slave trade to an end. He wrote hundreds of letters to those in authority. He returned to London and spoke to people in the government and gradually people listened. In time the slave trade was ended.

During his work of healing and teaching, David travelled to parts of Africa where no white man had ever been before. Livingstone knew how to make maps of all his journeys and so he began to open up a whole new continent. Livingstone was the first white man to see the great Victoria Falls and he named them after Queen Victoria.

David Livingstone was not always well himself. He caught malaria, which was very common in that country, and although he carried medicines to treat himself, he was never really free from this illness. He died from malaria, and his body was brought home and buried in Westminster Abbey.

Livingstone gave all his life to serving Jesus without thinking of himself. Let us thank God for the example he set before us and let us continue to pray for the work of missionaries throughout the world.

Prayers

1   We thank you God for all the brave people who have given their lives in working for the good of all. May we have their spirit of adventure and dedication so that we may in our turn be of some use in the world. Amen.

2   O God our Father we ask you to bless all missionaries in their work overseas. Help them as they face each new day. Bless their own families and all the people in your great family whom they have chosen to serve. Amen.

3   We praise your name, O God.
    For all who have spread the good news of the gospel
    throughout the world,
    For all who have faced the dangers of untrodden paths
    and unknown peoples,
    For all who have worked to free the slaves and heal the
    sick,
    We praise you, O God, for all who have laboured in
    our own land or overseas to make your kingdom come
    on earth. Amen.

Hymns

Jesus shall reign where'er the sun (WCV 67)
Far round the world thy children sing (WCV 71)

~ ~ ~ ~ ~ ~ ~ ~ ~ ~ ~ ~

M is for Moses

The baby in the bullrushes

The Hebrew people were slaves in the land of Egypt. They
were not treated well and their lives were often very
unhappy. They had to work hard for the Egyptians and
they were often beaten and left short of food. They tried to
free themselves but they were without a leader and not
strong enough. When the men rebelled, Pharoah found
another cruel way to reduce their strength. He ordered
that every baby boy born to a Hebrew mother was to be
killed at birth. Some babies managed to escape this dreadful death. But Pharaoh realised baby boys were still
growing up in Hebrew homes, so then he ordered that
every baby Hebrew boy was to be thrown into the River
Nile. He sent his soldiers round to the houses to make
sure his orders were carried out. Hebrew families tried to
hide their baby boys and keep them safe. But the soldiers
were ruthless. They searched the homes, they listened for
the sound of a baby's cry and they took away all the little
boys they found.

One Hebrew mother in Egypt was determined to protect her tiny son. She planned a clever way to safeguard
him. She knew he would not be safe in the house, for the
soldiers would search every corner. So she began to weave
a cradle with reeds from the river bank. To be sure it
would float safely and let in no water, she covered her

little cradle with clay and tar to make it watertight. (Exodus 2: 1–10)

When it was ready, the mother placed her baby in his little bed of reeds and she carried it down to the water's edge and hid it in the water among the reeds. She told her daughter Miriam to stay close to the river, and then she would be able to keep watch over the cradle and see what happened to it.

Presently Pharaoh's daughter came down to the river to bathe, accompanied by her ladies-in-waiting. The princess soon noticed the little basket among the reeds and sent one of her ladies-in-waiting to see what it was. When the basket was brought to the princess, she lifted the lid and there lay the baby. "Why," she said, "it is a little Hebrew boy." She decided to keep the baby and bring him up as her own child in the palace.

Miriam, the baby's sister, had watched all that was happening with wonder. She saw the princess look lovingly at her brother and she knew that the baby would be safe. Miriam ran to the princess and asked her if she could find a nurse for the baby from among the Hebrew mothers. Pharaoh's daughter agreed to this suggestion, so Miriam went and called her own mother and brought her to the princess. The princess said to the mother, "Take this child and look after him for me. I will pay you for the work you do. When he is old enough you must bring him to me." So the baby's own mother took him home and loved him and cared for him and when the little boy was old enough she took him to the palace. Pharaoh's daughter adopted the child and called him Moses.

So Moses was brought up in the palace of the Pharaoh of Egypt who ruled over the Hebrews with such cruelty. One day when Moses was grown up he went out and saw how badly the Egyptians behaved towards the Hebrews. He saw the heavy work the Hebrews had to do. He saw an Egyptian whip one of the Hebrew slaves. Moses knew then that he had been saved from the river for a special purpose. God had chosen him to lead the Hebrews out of Egypt to a land of freedom. It was going to take Moses all his life to accomplish this task and even though he lived to a very great age he never reached the promised land. But he brought his people very close and they were able to go on without him across the River Jordan. Much happened to Moses on the great journey through which he led his people. God guided and directed Moses all the time. The Hebrew people mourned for Moses when he died, for they remembered then what life had been like for them when they were slaves.

Prayers

1 O God our Father we thank you that you take care of us at all times and in all places. Just as you protected the baby Moses as he lay alone in his cradle on the water, so you will always be with us. We need fear no evil, if we put our trust in you. Amen.

2 All our loved ones we commend,
Lord, to you, man's truest friend,
Guard and guide them to the end,
We beseech you, Jesus. Amen.

3 We thank you God our Father for the shelter and comfort of our homes, for the love and companionship of family and friends, and for all the blessings which we take so much for granted. Please bless all those whose home life is not secure; children left as orphans, refugees who must leave all behind them. Help us to reach out in love to those in need. Amen.

Hymns

Father hear the prayer we offer (WCV 26)
Praise the Lord, ye heavens adore him (CP 35)

~ ~ ~ ~ ~ ~ ~ ~ ~ ~ ~ ~

M is for Mothers

Mothers' love

I will read you a little poem this morning, which reminds us how much our mothers love us, even when we have been very naughty. The poem is called *My mother's love*.

I didn't want a bath last night
But Mummy said I should,
I grumbled and was very slow,
And wasn't very good.

I said, "The water's much too hot,"
I said, "The soap's got lost,"
(I'd really broken it in half
Just to make Mummy cross).

I put the flannel up the taps,
I tipped up the shampoo,
I used my sister's bubble bath
And talcum powder, too.

Mummy came in, she was quite cross,
And I was very glad,
I wanted her to be upset,
I'd tried to make her sad.

It served her right for saying
I'd got to go to bed,
She dried me without speaking,
She only shook her head.

I hurried into bed last night,
I didn't want a book,
I didn't want a good-night kiss,
I wouldn't even look.

"Goodnight, my love," my Mummy said,
"And don't be cross for long,
However much you don't like me,
I love you all along.

I love you just like breathing,
It goes on night and day.
And when you wake tomorrow
You'll feel better straight away."

Mothering Sunday

Mothering Sunday falls in the middle of Lent and has another name, too, which is "Refreshment Sunday". The custom started many years ago, when young men who had left their homes to find work returned on this special Sunday to visit their mothers. They took gifts for their mothers and they would all go to church to thank God for bringing all the family together again. The mothers would bake a special cake to be eaten that day and this was called a simnel cake. This is a lovely fruit cake with marzipan in the centre. Sometimes we see cakes like this on sale at

Easter time, but the proper occasion for eating a simnel cake is on Mothering Sunday. Today, we still like to go to church as a family on this day and in many churches children are given cards, or posies of flowers, to give to their mothers. When we do this we are keeping alive an old custom.

Prayers

1   Lord Jesus, hear our thankfulness,
And with your love our mothers bless;
May we love them as we should,
And show our love, by being good. Amen.

2   O Lord our Heavenly Father, we ask for your blessing on our homes and families. We thank you for our mothers and fathers and all those who love us and take care of us. Help us to try and help them and grant that we may all love and serve you more and more. Through Jesus Christ our Lord. Amen.

3   May the love of God our Father
Be in all our homes today;
May the love of the Lord Jesus
Keep our heart and minds always:
May his loving Holy Spirit
Guide and bless the ones we love,
Fathers, mothers, brothers, sisters,
Keep them safely in his love. Amen.

Hymns

Tell out my soul the greatness of the Lord (100 HT 89)
O God in heaven whose loving plan (100 HT 74)

~ ~ ~ ~ ~ ~ ~ ~ ~ ~ ~ ~ ~

M is for Music

Handel's Messiah

I am sure that you all enjoy listening to music. We are fortunate nowadays because we can hear music whenever we wish. People who write music are called composers and this morning we are going to hear about one in particular. His name was Handel and he wrote many well-known pieces of music. He wrote the "Messiah", in which

113

he set to music some of the Old Testament readings foretelling the birth of Christ. Handel wrote this music just before he began to lose his sight, and he did not leave his study from the day he started to compose until twenty-four days later, when the great work was finished. It was a wonderful achievement.

The "Messiah" was performed in London in 1743 in front of an audience including King George II. The king stood to attention as the "Hallelujah Chorus" was played. He did so as a sign of respect and ever since that time, people have stood up to listen to the Hallelujah Chorus. When Handel was writing this music it gave him great joy. He said to his faithful servant, Smith, "I did think that I saw all heaven before me, and the great God himself. As the music went on to the paper, choirs of angels with glad eyes sang the 'Hallelujah Chorus'." Our lives have been made richer by this, and other wonderful pieces of music composed by Handel.

Prayers

1 O God, our Father, we praise you this morning for the gift of music and for ears to hear the wonderful sounds of great orchestras and simple instruments. We thank you for great composers who have written down their music for all to enjoy and for modern inventions that bring it to us again and again. Amen.

2 Thank you, God, for the gift of music. May we not neglect it, but use its power and beauty to lead us nearer to yourself. Whether we sing, or play, or listen, and whether the music is a hymn or a song or a symphony, may we be blessed through this gift of yours, and cherish it always. Amen.

3 Children of the heavenly King,
As you journey sweetly sing;
Sing your saviour's worthy praise,
Glorious in his works and ways. Amen.

Hymns

Bursting into life (SM 31)
Praise the Lord in the rhythm of your music (CP 33)

~ ~ ~ ~ ~ ~ ~ ~ ~ ~ ~ ~

114

N is for Naaman

Naaman is cured of leprosy

Naaman was a captain in the King of Syria's army. He was a brave and fearless soldier and an excellent leader. His men liked him very much, for he was kind and just. The king was very pleased with Naaman because he had served him well and had won many battles. The king did not want to lose such a good soldier, but Naaman knew he would not be able to stay in the king's army much longer, because he had caught leprosy.

At first his illness was not too bad. Naaman had a few sore places on his legs and arms, but he knew he was getting worse. His legs and arms were beginning to feel numb, and the sores were spreading. There was no cure for leprosy in those days and although Naaman had seen the doctors and done everything he could to stop the disease spreading, he could not get better.

Naaman was sad because he liked his work. He dreaded the day when he would have to give it up and go and live on his own as all lepers had to when their illness got very bad. Other people were afraid of catching it, so those who had leprosy were sent away until they died. Naaman's wife, too, was filled with sorrow. She knew her husband was ill and there was nothing she could do to make him better. Naaman's wife had a little maid servant who had been taken from her home in Israel and sold as a slave. Before she had left her home, the little girl had been taught about the Lord God. She, with her parents, had listened to the words of the great prophets and she worshipped the God of the Jews. She had been very kindly treated by Naaman and his wife, so when Naaman became ill she was sad. One day she said to her mistress, "If only my master could meet the prophet who lives in Samaria, he would get rid of the disease for him." (2 Kings 5: 3) She told Naaman's wife about the prophet, Elisha, who was in Israel and who had done some wonderful things through prayer.

When Naaman got to hear of all this, he went to the King of Syria and told him what his wife's maid had said. The king said that Naaman should go to Israel and try to get help, and he gave Naaman a letter to give to the King of Israel. So Naaman and some of his own servants prepared for the journey and Naaman took with him some fine presents. As soon as they were ready they left their own country and Naaman went straight away to the King of Israel and gave him the letter. The king opened it. The letter said, "This letter is to inform you that I am sending to you my servant Naaman, and I beg you to rid him of his disease." (2 Kings 5: 6) The King of Israel was very worried because he did not know how he could possibly cure Naaman's illness. He wondered if the King of Syria wanted to quarrel with him. He did not want to go to war against the Syrians. The King of Israel did not know what to do.

When Elisha, the prophet, heard what had happened, he sent a message to the king saying, "Let the man come to me." So Naaman went to Elisha's house. When he arrived, Elisha did not go out to greet him. Instead he sent a messenger to Naaman saying, "If you will go and wash seven times in the River Jordan, your flesh will be restored and you will be clean." When Naaman received this message he was furious. He thought Elisha was making fun of him. He turned round in anger, prepared to go straight back home. But one of Naaman's servants came up to him and said, "If the prophet had ordered you to do something difficult, would you not do it? Then should you not go and wash and be cured willingly?"

Naaman realised he was acting in a foolish, sulky way. All he really wanted was to be cured of his leprosy. His anger died down and he went to the river Jordan. His servants followed, and Naaman went and dipped himself in the Jordan seven times, just as Elisha had instructed him. When he had done this, he came out of the water. The sores on his body had miraculously disappeared. Naaman looked and felt better than he had done for a very long time. The first thing he wanted to do was to go back to Elisha and thank him with all his heart. He came to Elisha and said, "Now I know there is no other god but the one true God whom you serve. From this moment on I will worship none other." Then Naaman begged Elisha to accept the rich gifts he had brought for him. But Elisha refused them all. He explained to Naaman that it was not his own power which had healed Naaman, but the power of God working through him. Naaman understood and Elisha told him to return to his home in peace.

It must have been a wonderful moment for Naaman's wife, and for the little maid when they saw the captain of the army returning home well, and with the power of a new faith.

Prayers

1 We thank you God that we have healthy minds and healthy bodies. May we grow stronger and more reliable in your care. Amen.

2 O God help us not to be angry without cause. Make us ready to control our tempers, so that we can see the right way. Help us not to act in haste and then regret what we have done. Amen.

3 O Lord God, help us to be humble. Teach us obedience. Show us our need of you. Help us to feel your presence in our lives. For Jesus's sake. Amen.

Hymns

Through the night of doubt and sorrow (WCV 53)
Remember all the people (WCV 70)

~ ~ ~ ~ ~ ~ ~ ~ ~ ~ ~ ~

N is for Nature

The legend of Caedmon

When we think about nature we think of the beautiful world that God has created for us. The sky and the sea, the hills, the woods and the fields, the parks and gardens, the trees and flowers and birds and animals and insects.

There is a wonderful story about a man who lived hundreds of years ago, who learnt to sing about God's great creations. He worshipped God by setting to music the glories of nature and singing God's praises. Through this great gift he helped others to praise and glorify God too.

The man's name was Caedmon and he worked in the grounds of an abbey. The abbey was in Whitby in Yorkshire and the Abbess Hilda was in charge of the monks and nuns who lived there. Caedmon was not a monk and he could not read or write. He was a cowman who looked after the cattle and milked the cows. If he had any spare time he also helped on the farm and in the gardens.

Caedmon went contentedly about his duties day in, day out. It was a life of hard work but he enjoyed it and the days passed peacefully. The workers would often gather together in the evenings and entertain each other with stories and music. There was no television or radio in those days and people had to make their own entertainment. One evening, the crowd was jollier than usual. Someone had brought a harp, and this was being passed round. Everyone in turn was expected to sing or play to entertain the others. Caedmon was very shy. He could not play a musical instrument and certainly he could not sing. He knew he would never be able to entertain the company, so he slipped away. Nobody noticed his going. He was not an important person among them, he was only the cowherd. Caedmon went to the cowshed to be alone. Glad to have found a quiet place on his own, he lay down on some straw in the cowshed and fell asleep.

It was very still and quiet when Caedmon woke up to hear someone calling his name. "Caedmon, Caedmon, will you sing for me?" said the voice. Caedmon felt sure it was God himself, or one of his angels, speaking to him. He answered fearfully, "My Lord, I cannot sing." "Caedmon, you shall sing for me," said the Lord "and I will help." "But what shall I sing?" asked Caedmon. "I know no songs." "If you love me, Caedmon, sing of my world. Sing of the creation, sing of the beauty of the world that lies about you. Sing of all the glorious things the Lord God has made. Sing of the one who made heaven and earth. Sing of God in his glory." Caedmon had received his answer. He opened his mouth and began to sing. At first his voice was a bit weak and shaky, but it grew stronger. Words came into his head and he sang songs of glory. "O praise the eternal God who made such marvels," rang out the rich voice of Caedmon. People stopped to listen. They heard Caedmon's wonderful voice singing the praises of the Lord and they went with haste to pass on the news to the Abbess Hilda.

The Abbess sent for Caedmon and made him sing for her. "This is a gift sent from God," she said. She told one of the monks to teach Caedmon stories from the Bible. Caedmon put the stories into verse and then set them to music. And so Caedmon became one of the earliest poets. At Whitby, the place where Caedmon sang to the glory of

God, there is still a stone which has been placed in his memory. On it are written some lines, which may have been composed by Caedmon himself.

Praise we loudly the Lord of heaven,
Praise His wisdom and wonderful power,
The glorious works of the great creator,
The Father eternal who founded the world,
See, he set for the sons of men
A heaven high to roof them in.

Prayers

1 Father, we thank you for all your gifts;
For the life-giving sun and the life-giving rain,
For the woods and fields,
For the flowers and birds
For the rivers and the sea,
For the hills and valleys,
And for the glory of the open sky.
For eyes to see and health to enjoy,
Everything around us rejoices.
Make us also to rejoice
And give us thankful hearts. Amen.

2 Heavenly Father, thank you for the beauty and wonder and richness that the world of nature provides for us. Amen.

3 O God who has given us eyes to see
The beauty that is here and there,
Give us a heart to find out thee,
And see your presence everywhere. Amen.

Hymns

Praise the Lord, ye heavens adore him (WCV 16)
O praise him, O praise him (CP 13)

~ ~ ~ ~ ~ ~ ~ ~ ~ ~ ~ ~ ~

N is for Night

The Red Indian's test of manhood

God is our Father. He loves us and protects us. He is always with us when we are in dangerous or difficult situations. Listen to this story about a young Red Indian boy, and it will help you to understand that you need never fear.

When young Red Indian boys were approaching manhood there were many tests of ability and courage which they had to pass. One boy had completed nearly all of them and he was about to face the last round of trials. He was very anxious to do well, because he wanted to become a man. He was a good hunter and he wanted to go hunting with the men instead of staying with the women and children at the camp. The young Indian did not know exactly what he would be asked to do in the final test. His father came to him and said he was to go with him that night, instead of going to sleep, and his last test would take place. As evening came, father and son set out together. They walked a long way into the deep forest, creeping stealthily, for there were wild animals about. The forest was thick and the night was pitch black. The father touched his son and they both stopped. He spoke to the young boy and gave him his instructions. He said, "I am going back to the camp now. You must stay here alone, all night, and keep guard. When it is light I shall come for you again." Then the father turned round and left his son to keep watch on his own through the long hours of the night.

Now the young Indian boy understood how his courage was being tested. He longed to creep quietly back to the camp behind his father. He wished his older brother were there to talk to and to share the long hours of the night ahead. He did not know whether the strange noises around him were only the movement of wind or leaves and twigs or whether a wild animal was approaching. Many worries and fears went through his mind as, little by little, the hours of darkness passed and a faint morning light appeared at last in the sky. As the sky grew lighter, the trees stood out clearly again. As he gazed about him, the young man was surprised to see his father walking towards him, coming to fetch him, as he had promised he would when the light of day dawned. "Father," said the young Indian, "you have arrived so suddenly. I expected you to come from further away." "Son," replied his father, "I have watched with you all night. I did not go back to the camp as I told you I would. Do you see that great tree? I

120

was behind it all night. If any terrible thing had happened to you, I would have been close by to help. But you have proved that you are brave and fearless. Come now. We will return to the camp together."

So the father and his son went back to the camp. The young Indian was now a man and his father was very proud of him. But let us remember that the young Indian was never really on his own and he need have had no fear. We are like that boy, and God is our father, close beside us at all times.

Prayers

1   Father we thank Thee for the night,
And for the pleasant morning light,
For rest and food and loving care
And all that makes the day so fair. Amen.

2   For the silvery moon and twinkling stars
that make the night so beautiful,
We thank you heavenly Father.
For the quietness and restfulness of the night,
We thank you heavenly Father.
For our warm beds and loving homes,
We thank you heavenly Father.
For our parents and all those we love,
We thank you heavenly Father. Amen.

3   Lord keep us safe at night,
Secure from all our fears.
May angels guard us while we sleep,
Till morning light appears. Amen.

4   Lighten our darkness Lord, we pray; and in your mercy defend us from all perils and dangers of this night; for the love of your only son, our Saviour, Jesus Christ. Amen.

O Lord, support us all the day long of this troubled
5   life, till the shades lengthen, and the evening comes, and the busy world is hushed, the fever of life is over, and our work is done. Then, Lord, in your mercy, grant us safe lodging, a holy rest and peace at the last. Amen.

Hymns
My Father for another night (WCV 1)
Now the day is over (WCV 14)

~ ~ ~ ~ ~ ~ ~ ~ ~ ~ ~ ~

N is for Noah

Noah's ark

Noah trusted God and always obeyed his commands. When God told him to build a huge boat, an ark, he did so straight away. God told Noah just how it should be made. He told Noah that there would be a great flood which would cover all the earth and that the ark would be a safe place. Noah was to take on board the ark his wife, his three sons and their wives and a male and female of each kind of bird, beast and reptile. He was also to take all the food that this strange group of people and animals would need whilst they lived in the ark. Noah carefully carried out all God's commands, for he believed that the flood would come as God had warned. God promised that Noah and all the people and animals who went with him into the ark would be kept safe for the forty days and forty nights that the rains would last.

Noah and his sons worked hard. They began to load the ark as soon as it was ready to carry all the animals. When the rains began to fall, and after all the creatures had gone into the ark he entered with his wife, his sons and their wives. Once they were all safely inside the rain began to come down hard. It rained without stopping for forty days. It must have seemed a very long time to Noah and his family, as well as to all the animals, as they lived crowded together in their strange home. But the ark floated safely on the surface of the water and nobody inside it came to any harm. Even when the rains stopped, it was many more days before the flood began to go down.

After a hundred and fifty days the ark came to rest on the top of Mount Ararat. Then Noah opened a trapdoor and let out a raven. The raven flew over the earth until it found a new place to build a nest but it did not come back to Noah. When Noah had waited for another seven days he sent out a dove. The dove could find nowhere to rest so she came back to the ark. Seven days later, he let the dove go again. Again she returned to Noah, but this time the bird had an olive branch in her beak. This was a sign to Noah that the waters were going down and the tops of the trees were appearing again. Noah waited another seven days and he let the dove go for a third time. The dove did not return to the ark again. Then Noah was sure if was safe at last to open the door. So Noah came out with his sons, his wife and his sons' wives, followed by the animals, birds and reptiles. (Genesis 8: 16–19)

The first thing that Noah did when he was safely on dry land again was to build an altar and kneel in thanksgiving to God, who had kept them all safe through the days of the flood. God spoke again to Noah. He told Noah that he and his sons would continue to have charge over all the animals they had cared for during the flood. God promised that there would never be another flood like the one which had covered all the earth and he put a rainbow in the sky as a sign of this promise.

Prayers

1 O God, we thank you that you send both sun and rain to the earth. We thank you for all your creatures which inhabit the earth with us. Help us to remember that we must do our part to care for and protect all your creation. Amen.

2 Dear God, whenever we see your rainbow in the sky, we are reminded of your promise to take care of us each day. Help us to keep the promises which we make to you, to our parents and to our friends. We ask this in Jesus' name. Amen.

3 God sends the sunshine and the rain
To make us think, along the way,
That life with all its ups and downs,
Is like a changing April day.
It's easy to be happy, through all the sunny hours,
But we must learn to smile and sing
When sunshine turns to showers. Amen.

Hymns

Have you heard the raindrops (CP 2)
Who put the colours in the rainbow (CP 12)

~ ~ ~ ~ ~ ~ ~ ~ ~ ~ ~ ~

N is for Nurses

Florence Nightingale

Florence Nightingale was born in Florence in Italy, where her parents were living at the time. Her parents were wealthy, well educated people. She was brought up in the gentle manner of girls at that time. Nobody expected that she would train for a job, or that she would take up any work when she was old enough. Ladies had only to be gentle, polite and able to run the household and care for the needs of a husband and children.

The first time she went to visit a hospital she was appalled to discover what a dirty and depressing place it was. People who went into hospital did not expect to come out alive. The nurses had no training. They knew nothing about hygiene or care of the sick. They were themselves poor and ignorant people. Florence was filled with a burning desire to train as a nurse and do really useful work in a hospital where she could make the changes that were urgently needed. But Florence's parents would not allow her to do that, as they thought that nursing was not a suitable occupation for a young lady. Florence did not give up easily though. She was determined that one day she would achieve her ambition. She studied from books, gaining all the medical knowledge she could, and whenever one of her relatives was ill she was eager to help. In the end her parents allowed her to train as a nurse.

By the time Florence Nightingale was qualified, Britain, France and Turkey were at war with Russia. The Crimean war, as it was called, broke out in 1854 and many fierce battles were fought. Many wounded soldiers died because they did not receive proper treatment. The French provided hospitals and nursing care for their wounded soldiers, but very little was done by the British for their soldiers. News began to reach home about this awful state of affairs. The Minister of War, who knew about Florence Nightingale, decided to write and ask her if she would lead a group of women to go and nurse the wounded soldiers. Before the Minister's letter had arrived, Florence had already volunteered her services. She interviewed many women before she chose the forty who were to go with her. Many of those she took were nuns who wanted to serve God through their devotion to those most in need of help.

It was hard, demanding work that needed great determination and courage. There were some doctors at work in the Crimea who resented Florence and her nurses interfering. But nothing could stop Florence. She helped to scrub floors, wash sheets, and care for the dying. She and her nurses brought order to the hospitals.

Their care and devotion was rewarded. Soldiers who had been dying began to recover. Their wounds were washed and bandaged so they did not get further infection. Their dirty beds on the floor were cleaned. Their food was improved. As the sick men began to get well their love for Florence Nightingale and her nurses grew. Reports of Florence's work reached Britain. The government no longer felt ashamed of the way the soldiers were being treated. Queen Victoria was greatly impressed by all that Florence Nightingale had done. She wrote to Florence saying, "I know of the Christian devotion which you have shown during the war. I need hardly tell you how warm my admiration is for your services, which is fully equal to those of my brave soldiers."

Florence Nightingale's work was now fully recognised. The soldiers called her "The lady with the lamp" because at night she would walk round the wards with her lamp, checking that all was well with each of her patients. But the end of the war was not the end of Florence Nightingale's work. Although she became ill herself and never fully recovered, Florence Nightingale brought about great nursing reforms in the hospitals of our country. Nursing became a proud and noble profession. So if ever you have to go to hospital, be thankful for the hard and devoted work of the nurses and remember the lady of the lamp who did so much to help sick people regain their health.

Prayers

1   Thank you, God, for all the nurses and doctors who help the sick and suffering. May we always be grateful to them. Amen.

2 O Lord Jesus Christ, tend your sick ones. Rest your weary ones. Bless your dying ones. Soothe your suffering ones. Pity your afflicted ones and shield your joyous ones. All this for your sake. Amen.

3 Lord Jesus Christ, we pray today for all nurses who are carrying out their duties in hospitals, nursing homes and private homes in our own country and overseas. Be with them as they go about their work and bless them in the care they give to the sick. May we, like them, find a way to be of service as we go through life. Amen.

Hymns

O God whose will is life and good (100 HT 75)
He gave me eyes (CP 18)

~ ~ ~ ~ ~ ~ ~ ~ ~ ~ ~ ~ ~

O is for Obstacles
Thalidomide children

Obstacles are difficulties that we have to overcome. But obstacles have their useful purpose, too. If we never met any obstacles, we would never learn to be brave, we would never learn to be strong in mind and spirit, we would never be able to be proud of overcoming difficulties. Sometimes we grumble about things not being fair. But some people with terrible obstacles in their lives are so brave that they make us feel very humble and ashamed that we ever complain. We all complain sometimes, but if you think about some of the people I'm going to talk about today, perhaps you will think twice before you have your next big grumble.

Not very many years ago a new medicine was manufactured. Doctors thought it would be a great help and many people took it. Unfortunately the drug had a terrible effect on babies and many were born with dreadful handicaps. When people realised the new medicine was the cause, nobody was given any more tablets. But by that time there were many "thalidomide babies". Some of these children were born without arms or hands, or had hands but no fingers, or did not have properly formed legs. Sometimes their feet were the wrong way round. All these poor handicapped children had to have many operations and some could never be completely cured. They had to learn to manage the best they could. Some of these thalidomide children turned out to be very inventive. Although they had so many obstacles, those without hands learnt to use their feet in a way which you and I would have thought quite impossible. Those without feet could make their wheel-chairs do fantastic things. Now many of these children have grown up and do jobs. If they had just sat down and felt sorry for themselves this would have been impossible. Quite recently on the television there was a film about a mother without arms, who had had a baby. She did everything for her baby with her feet. She could even bath him and change his nappies. I shall never forget that film because the mother was so clever and brave in all that she had learnt to do. She had overcome great obstacles.

We do not know what obstacles we may meet in life. Let

us ask for God's help to meet all our obstacles bravely so that each one becomes a challenge to us.

Prayers

1 Dear Lord Jesus, you know what obstacles we must face each day. Help us to face each one with courage, prepared to follow in the footsteps of all those who have been brave in face of many difficulties. Amen.

2 We remember before you, O Lord, all who are handicapped through no fault of their own. Those who have lost their health and strength, the blind, the deaf, the dumb; those who suffer because of racial prejudice, those who have unhappy home backgrounds. Help them, we pray, through all their obstacles and show them that there can never be a crown without a cross. Amen.

3 Through all the changing scenes of life,
In trouble and in joy,
The praises of my God shall still
My heart and tongue employ. Amen.

Hymns

Lead us heavenly Father lead us (WCV 56)
Thine by the glory (100 HT 95)

~ ~ ~ ~ ~ ~ ~ ~ ~ ~ ~ ~ ~

O is for Offero

The legend of St Christopher

There was once a very strong young man called Offero, who wanted to use all his strength to serve the most powerful person he could find. So Offero joined the king's army and fought many battles. For some years he was happy until he discovered that this king feared an even more powerful and evil king. Offero set off to find this evil king and to offer to serve him. He wanted to serve only someone as strong as himself. In the depths of a black forest Offero found the evil king and joined his army. He stayed with the evil king for some years. But one day when they were out riding together, they came across a large wooden cross on a hillside. The evil king turned pale and shook with fear. He rode off in a different direction with Offero in hot pursuit. "You are the bravest man in the world," cried Offero, "and you fear a cross of wood!" "No," replied the evil king, "it is not the cross I fear, but the one who died upon it."

Offero left the evil king, determined to find out more about the one who had died on the cross. His power must be great indeed, if the evil king trembled at the thought of it. But Offero could not find the Lord, no matter where he searched. One wise man suggested he became a monk. He said that by serving the Lord in a monastery he would come to know God better. But Offero was certain this was not the right way for him. He was sure his gift of strength was meant to be used in the world around him. So he kept searching for ways to serve this great God. Finally he was given a very humble task, but one which only a strong person could undertake. He became a ferryman. He built himself a strong boat for carrying his passengers, for the river had many fierce currents. Then he built himself a hut near the river bank so that anyone who needed to cross the river had only to knock on his door.

One night there was a terrible storm. Offero settled down in his hut, certain that no one would want to cross the river. But he was suddenly disturbed by a knocking at the door and a voice crying out, "Offero, please will you take me over the river?" Offero went to the door and was amazed to see the figure of a child in the light of his lamp. "The storm is very bad," he said. "Come in and shelter in the hut. When it is calmer I will take you to the other side." "But I must cross tonight," insisted the child, and there was something about him which made Offero obey. "I cannot take my boat out on a night like this," he said, "but I will carry you over the river." Then he lifted the child onto his shoulders and set off into the raging waters of the river. At first, the child on his shoulders seemed no weight to the powerful Offero, but as he struggled against the raging currents of the river, the child seemed to grow heavier and heavier. Offero began to be afraid that he might not reach the opposite bank. But eventually he clambered onto the other side and gently lifted the child down from his shoulders. "I do not understand," he said, "how your weight proved so great. Every bit of my strength has been tested." "That is true, Offero," replied

129

the child. "You have carried on your shoulders the one who bears the weight of the whole world. Because you have always served the weak and because you have carried in your arms Christ himself, from now on you shall be called Christopher, which means the "Christ-bearer".

When he had said this, the child disappeared. But straight away the storm died down and everywhere was filled with a strange and radiant light. Then Christopher knew for certain that he was in the service of the most powerful person of all, and joyfully he prepared to serve this great king for the rest of his days.

Prayers

1   Dear Lord Jesus, help us to use the special gifts that you have given to each one of us in your service all the days of our lives. Amen.

2   Jesus, friend of the friendless, helper of the poor, healer of the sick, whose life was spent in doing good, let us follow in your footsteps. Make us strong to do right, gentle with the weak, and kind to all who are in sorrow, that we may be like you, our Lord and Master. Amen.

3   Teach us, O God, to learn how to use all our growing strength for the good of each other. Prepare our hearts and minds for the tasks that lie ahead, and so bring us to know the true happiness that comes through working for you. Amen.

Hymns

Travel on, travel on (CP 42)
At the name of Jesus (CP 58)

~ ~ ~ ~ ~ ~ ~ ~ ~ ~ ~ ~ ~

O is for Orphans
Gladys Aylward

Gladys Aylward was a maid in a big London house. She was sure God wanted her to go to China, to tell the people there about Christianity and so she went to one of the missionary societies and asked for work. But the people who interviewed Gladys did not think she would make a good missionary, so they said "No". Gladys was not put off. She found out what it would cost to buy a single ticket to China. It cost an enormous amount of money but Gladys began to save from her very small earnings. Eventually Gladys had the £50 she needed. She bought her own ticket and set out for China, in obedience to God's will. There was a lady in China whom Gladys knew and together they opened an inn for travellers. It was a simple place, but rest, food and shelter were provided and Gladys used to tell her visitors stories about Jesus.

The people of China were very poor. There were many beggars. Children wandered about in ragged clothes with no one to care for them. Many of them were orphans. One mother begged Gladys to buy her little girl from her. Gladys was deeply saddened by all that she saw around her and so she took into her inn many children who had no home. Soon she had a hundred orphans in her care and then another terrible thing happened. War broke out between China and Japan and the town where Gladys Aylward had her children's home was no longer safe. She knew she would have to take her children away. They must get over to the other side of the mountains and across the great river to safety. There was no one to help Gladys. Some of the children were very small. It was a long, long way to go. Where would they rest? What would they do about food on the journey? How would they cross the river if they ever reached it? Would the walk over the mountains be too far for the little ones? Gladys asked God for help in her prayers.

When she had prayed, Gladys was certain that she and her large family had to set out on that journey. The children went early to bed that night, to be well rested for the next day and two young men came from the ruler of the town with food for the children, which they offered to carry. The journey was long and tiring. The mountain paths were steep. The children's legs ached, some of them got blisters, but still they went on. One night a Buddhist priest let them all sleep in his temple. Throughout the journey Gladys asked God for guidance. She encouraged the tired children. She kept them as cheerful as she could, and her strength gave them courage. She was very tired herself but she thought only of the little orphans whom she had to get to safety. At last they reached the river.

Now another problem faced Gladys: how to cross the river. There were some Chinese soldiers nearby and Gladys asked if they could provide a boat to take them over the water. They said it was impossible. The children were beginning to cry and wanted to know what was happening. "There is no boat," Gladys told them gently. "We have no way of crossing the river." The children said at once, "But won't God help us to cross? God made sure that Moses passed safely through the sea." "You are right," said Gladys. "We shall pray together and God will show us a way." So the weary travellers knelt down and each one asked God for help. When they opened their eyes they witnessed a miracle. The soldiers had changed their minds. One of them had gone and fetched a boat and there was the transport that they needed. With one voice they shouted, "Thank God" and Gladys and all her children crossed safely over the river and made for the nearest town.

There they settled, but at first Gladys was too ill to care for the children herself. She had almost killed herself in taking them to safety. She proved to the whole world that her faith and her trust in God were absolute and that God himself had helped her carry out the work he had chosen for her.

Prayers

1   O Lord, we remember in our prayers this day, all the children of the world. Please help those who are hungry and comfort any who are lonely and afraid. We ask for your special blessing on all orphaned children and on those who love and care for them today. Amen.

2   Dear Lord Jesus, friend of little children, be near to all those who have lost the people they hold most dear. You are our Father and we know that we need never fear, for you will always be close to us. Amen.

3   We bring to you our praises,
Receive them, Lord, we pray
And bless all your dear children
At home and far away.
Lord, grant that soon your light may shine,
Wide over all this work of thine. Amen.

Hymns

Alleluya sing to Jesus (WCV 118)
Far round the world (WCV 71)

~ ~ ~ ~ ~ ~ ~ ~ ~ ~ ~ ~ ~ ~

P is for Parables
The lost coin

When Jesus wanted to teach the people and help them to understand what he was saying, he often told stories with a lesson in them. These are called parables.

One parable Jesus told was about a woman who had ten pieces of silver. This was her treasure and she took great care of it. One day she discovered that one silver coin was missing. She did everything she could to find it. She lit the lamp so that she could see better into all the dark corners. She took her broom and carefully brushed the floor, hoping that the piece of silver would be swept up from wherever it had rolled. She did not give up her search until at last she had found the piece that was lost. When all ten silver pieces were safely put away the woman called together her friends and neighbours. She told them how worried she had been and how pleased she was when she found the missing coin. "Rejoice with me! I have found the piece that I lost," she said. (Luke 15: 9) The joy that she felt was shared by all those around who knew and liked her. "And that," said Jesus, "is what it is like in the Kingdom of Heaven when one of us who has done wrong asks to be forgiven."

The sower and the seed

One day a very big crowd had gathered round Jesus and they all wanted to listen to his teaching. So he told them another parable. (Luke 8: 5–8) One day a sower went out to sow his seed. As he was scattering the seed some of it fell on the footpath. This seed was soon destroyed because either people trod on it or the birds swooped down and had a good feast. Some of the seed fell on hard, stony ground. This seed sprang up quickly, but because there was so little soil, the plants could not make strong roots. Plants need healthy roots to draw water, so once the seed had grown, it shrivelled and died because it could not get enough water. Some seed fell where there were lots of thistles and weeds and it was choked by the weeds. The rest of the seed fell on the good rich earth, where the ground had been prepared for it and the soil was ploughed and free from weeds. This seed grew well. It was strong and healthy and produced a plentiful crop, worth a hundred times what it had originally cost. Jesus finished the story by saying, "If you have ears to hear, then hear."

The disciples asked Jesus what the parable meant. He replied, "This is what the parable means. The seed is like the word of God. It is being given for all to receive. But the men who hear it and toss it aside in disbelief are like the pathway. The seed that falls on them is immediately taken by the birds. Other people may accept the word of God gladly, but at the first sign of difficulty they lose their faith. These people are like the stony ground. The seed cannot take root in them. Yet other people hear the word of God and accept it, and for a time they follow God's teachings. But then all the cares and worries and pleasures of life begin to take over again, and they forget about the things that matter most. Those people are like the ground which had thistles and weeds. But most of the seed fell on to the good soil. The good soil is like the people who have good and honest hearts and who persevere and always try to hold to their faith. They produce a good harvest." (Luke 8: 11–15)

We must try, in our lives, to prepare the soil around us well, so that our seed can grow and produce a good harvest.

Prayers

1 Dear God, help us to remember the teaching of Jesus. Make our lives rich in your service that we may produce a good harvest and give the glory to you, our Father. Amen.

2 Dear Lord Jesus, we like to listen to stories. Thank you for all the stories you have told to us. Help us to remember the lessons that you taught us as we live our lives each day. Amen.

3 Father in Heaven, bless your little children
Gathered before you on this holy day.
For the morning sunshine, for the day we thank you,
O Sun of Love, shine in our hearts we pray.

Father in Heaven, help your little children,
To please you always in their work and play,

135

Help them to be truthful, gentle, kind and loving,
To be like Jesus and follow him each day. Amen.

Hymns

There was a man on a long long journey-o (SM 23)
Every word comes alive (CP 72)

~ ~ ~ ~ ~ ~ ~ ~ ~ ~ ~ ~ ~

P is for Patrick

Patrick's life

Patrick is the patron saint of Ireland. His special day is 17
March. The people of Ireland honour St Patrick because he
worked very hard in their country to help people learn
about Jesus at a time when many of them were not
Christians.

Patrick was not born in Ireland and he was not at all
happy when he first went there. He did not go to Ireland
because he wanted to, or even because his family went to
live there. He was taken to Ireland as a slave. Some wild
pirates invaded the place where he lived and carried off
many of the people as prisoners to sell them as slaves.
Patrick was only sixteen years old when this happened
and he must have felt very homesick, lonely and miserable
in a foreign country away from all the people he had
known and loved. He had to work on a desolate mountain
farm looking after the sheep and the pigs. One night he
managed to escape and he made his way to the coast. It
was a long and difficult journey but Patrick was determined to leave Ireland.

When he got to the coast he found a ship that was about
to set sail. At first the captain refused to let Patrick go on
board, but he changed his mind at the last moment.
Joyfully Patrick watched the coast of Ireland disappearing
into the distance. He must have thought then that he
never wanted to see Ireland again. He was taken to France
and there he joined a monastery and trained to be a priest.
Patrick spent three years in France and then God spoke to
him and told him there was special work for him to do in
Ireland. The people of Ireland were without a Christian
leader, and they needed someone strong, yet kind, like
Patrick, who could teach them about Jesus and his love for
all the people. Patrick obeyed the voice of God and

136

prepared himself to spread the good news of Jesus to the Irish people. He knew his work would not be easy. He knew how wild and rough many of the Irishmen were. He knew that there were many who believed in the power of the heathen Druids, who would not want to listen to him. But Patrick was strong and brave in his faith and he and some helpers set off for Ireland, trusting in the power of God to care for them in all the dangers that lay ahead.

When they arrived, some people thought they were pirates and were prepared to attack them straight away. However, they found the strangers quiet, peaceful men. They put down their weapons and listened to Patrick and straight away some were baptised and became Christians. The chief in the town gave Patrick a barn to live in and it was there that Patrick held services. This became the first church in Ireland.

The legend of the Druids and the fire

There are many legends about Patrick's teaching in Ireland. There were many non-believers who did not accept his teaching, but he continued his work. One spring festival the followers of the Druids lit a great fire to drive away all evil spirits. They ordered that all other fires round about were to be put out. At the same time Patrick and his followers were preparing to celebrate the rising from the dead of Jesus Christ at Easter. Patrick wanted to show everyone that they should worship Jesus Christ, the Son of the one true God. So Patrick disobeyed the order and prepared his own fire. He built it high on a hill so that its light would be seen for miles around. When it was dark he lit it and the light from the flames shone over all the countryside around.

The Druids were angry and many of them set out to find Patrick and put him to death. Patrick spoke out boldly when he was questioned. "I am a torch bearer", he said, "and I bring the true light to lighten this dark land and to spread peace and goodwill." The Druids drew back from Patrick. They were afraid to harm him because he was so full of courage and sure of his faith, and many more became Christians.

1   O God, you gave to your servant, St Patrick, the fearless courage and strength to uphold his faith in all difficulties. Grant us to have the same faith, that we too may be prepared to acknowledge you at all times, through Jesus Christ our Lord. Amen.

2   Christ be with me, Christ within me,
    Christ behind me, Christ before me,
    Christ beside me, Christ to win me,
    Christ to comfort and restore me.
    Christ beneath me, Christ above me,
    Christ in quiet, Christ in danger,
    Christ in hearts of all that love me,
    Christ in mouth of friend and stranger. Amen.

3   May the strength of God pilot us,
    May the power of God preserve us,
    May the wisdom of God instruct us,
    May the hand of God protect us,
    Now and for evermore. Amen.

Hymns

Stand up, stand up for Jesus (WCV 49)
Glory be to thee my God (100 HT 30)

~ ~ ~ ~ ~ ~ ~ ~ ~ ~ ~ ~ ~

P is for Paul

Paul's conversion

On 25 January the church celebrates the conversion of St Paul. He was first known as Saul of Tarsus. Saul was not a Christian, he was one of the enemies of the Christian people and he persecuted those who believed in Jesus. He put people who preached about Christianity in prison and was even responsible for the death of some of them.

St Stephen was the first of the apostles to die for Jesus and Saul was there, watching, when Stephen was attacked and stoned to death. The Christians feared people like Saul, but they did not give up their faith even though Saul and other men made life so difficult for them. And yet Saul became a changed man. Jesus, through his Holy Spirit, brought about a miracle which changed his heart, and he became one of the first missionaries of the Church and one of its greatest leaders. (Acts 9: 1–30)

The apostles were moving from town to town spreading the good news of Jesus, and daily more and more new Christians were being baptised. This angered Saul and those in authority, so Saul asked for permission to go to Damascus to arrest any disciples who were still preaching about Jesus. Saul was on the road to Damascus, when suddenly "a light flashed from the sky." Saul fell to the ground. He heard a voice speaking, "Saul, Saul, why do you persecute me?" And Saul answered, "Tell me, Lord, who are you?" The voice replied, "I am Jesus, whom you are persecuting. Get up and go into the city, and you will be told what you have to do." The men who were travelling with Saul stood still in utter amazement. They heard the voice clearly, but they could not see anyone. Saul got to his feet, but although he opened his eyes he could no longer see. The men who were with him had to take his arm and guide him into Damascus. He stayed inside the house for three days. He was blind and he refused to have anything to eat or to drink.

There was already in Damascus a true disciple of Jesus, whose name was Ananias. One night he had a strange dream in which he heard the voice of the Lord speaking to him. "Ananias," said the Lord, "go at once to Straight Street, to the house of Judas, and ask for a man from Tarus, called Saul. You will find him praying, for he too has had a vision of a man called Ananias coming to him, and laying his hands upon him, and restoring his sight." But Ananias answered the Lord and protested, "Lord," he said, "I have heard about this man. I know of all the harm he has caused to your followers in Jerusalem. He has come here to arrest those who believe in you." But the Lord spoke again to Ananias and said, "You must go. He is the man I have chosen. He will spread my kingdom to many nations. I myself will show him all that he will have to go through for my sake."

Ananias knew then that the Lord had a special task for Saul and he set out to do as he had been told. He went to the house of Judas and found Saul. Ananias laid his hands on Saul and said to him, "Saul, my brother, the Lord Jesus who appeared to you on the way here, has sent me to you so that you may recover your sight, and be filled with the

Holy Spirit." When Ananias touched Saul, he immediately regained his sight. The first thing he asked for was to be baptised. Then he had some food and drink to help him regain his strength.

Paul's missionary work

After his baptism, the life of Saul was quite different. He changed his name to Paul and spent some time with the disciples in Damascus, learning more about the wonderful teaching of Jesus. Then Paul himself began to preach to the people and he astounded all those who gathered to hear him. "Isn't this the man who was in Jerusalem to destroy the Christians," they said. "Didn't he come here to arrest more of them?" They could not understand how Saul, who would not let anyone speak about Jesus, had become such a different person from this new Paul, who was now so strong and powerful in his teaching.

Later, Paul went on some long journeys with Barnabas and others. They had many adventures. Paul was shipwrecked, imprisoned and suffered a great deal for his faith. Yet he found joy in suffering for he said it brought him nearer to Jesus who had also suffered at the hands of his enemies. Because of Paul's great missionary work, the Christian faith began to spread throughout the world and the work that he began still continues.

Prayers

1   Almighty God, who caused the light of the gospel to shine throughout the world through the preaching of your servant, St Paul, grant that we who remember his wonderful conversion may follow him in bearing witness to your truth, through Jesus Christ our Lord. Amen.

2   We bring to you in prayer, O God, all missionaries who have left their homes to go to distant lands. Protect them in all danger and help them in all difficulties, so that they may never be lonely or afraid, because you are with them. For Jesus Christ's sake. Amen.

3   O Lord Jesus, you commanded that your apostles
should go into all the world to preach the gospel to
everyone. Let your name be great among all nations,
from the rising up of the sun to its going down. Amen.

Hymns

Fight the good fight (WCV 54)
Amazing grace, how sweet the sound (SM 47)

~ ~ ~ ~ ~ ~ ~ ~ ~ ~ ~ ~ ~

P is for Persistence

Robert Bruce

In 1306 Robert Bruce became King of Scotland. He had to
fight to keep his crown because the English did not want
the Scots to have their own king. The English invaded
Scotland and many Scots were taken as prisoners and
badly treated. Robert Bruce himself was lucky to escape,
and he went into hiding. He was very much afraid of what
was going to happen. The Scottish people had suffered
many defeats and Bruce felt unable to fight another battle.
He crept into a cave on a hillside to think how he could
escape from all his enemies who were gathering round.

It was cold and dark in the cave and Bruce sat hunched
up in the corner making his plans. Gradually he got used
to the half-light inside the cave and he began to look
around him. He noticed a spider making her web in the
corner of the roof of the cave. The spider was having a
difficult task. Each time she got a strand of her web from
one corner almost to another, it broke away. The spider
would start all over again, but the same thing kept
happening. She almost succeeded but at the last moment,
she failed. It seemed impossible to make a web in such a
difficult place. Bruce continued to watch the spider with
fascination. At each failed attempt he was certain the
spider would give up, but every time she went back to try
again. There seemed to be no limit to her patience and at
last her persistence was rewarded. The spider made her
web and settled down in it.

Robert Bruce thought about the spider. If such a little
creature could patiently try, try and try again, surely he
could summon up more courage and rally his army once
again to defeat the English. Bruce found a new determi-

nation to succeed and he was duly rewarded. At Bannock-
burn the two enemies met, and the English were defeated.

Prayers

1   O Lord, help us to work with persistence towards the
    goals that we most want to achieve. Amen.

2   Dear God we thank you for people of patience and
    understanding to whom we can talk and to whom we
    can take our problems. Teach us to know you, that we
    may bring to you in prayer all our hopes and fears, our
    difficulties and our doubts, our joys and our sorrows.
    Grant us your peace, through Christ our Lord. Amen.

3   Be our guide, O Lord, we pray
    Lest we stumble on the way.
    Be our strength, dear Lord, we ask
    As patiently we do each task. Amen.

Hymns

Father lead me day by day (WCV 27)
Jesus good above all other (WCV 43)

~ ~ ~ ~ ~ ~ ~ ~ ~ ~ ~ ~ ~

P is for Peter

Peter becomes a disciple

St Peter's Day is on 29 June. We can learn a lot about St
Peter's life from the New Testament. Until he met Jesus,
Peter was known to his friends as Simon, but Jesus gave
him the name "Peter", which was the Greek word for a
rock.

It was Andrew, Peter's brother, who introduced him to
Jesus. At that time Peter and Andrew were fishermen, but
Jesus said to the two brothers, "Come with me and I will
make you fishers of men." They left their nets at once and
followed him. (Matthew 4: 19–20) From that moment on,
Peter became one of the most faithful disciples and Jesus
loved him dearly. Peter was often present when Jesus
talked to the people and when he performed wonderful
miracles of healing. Peter told Jesus he loved him with all
his heart, and Jesus knew he would always be able to
depend on Peter.

Peter betrays Jesus

There were times though when Peter, like the rest of us, did things that he regretted. When Jesus told the disciples that one of them would betray him, all of them asked "Is it I?" Peter, however, was sure of his love for Jesus and he said with conviction, "Everyone else may fall away on your account, but I never will." (Matthew 26: 35) Jesus said to him in reply, "I tell you, tonight before the cock crows, you will disown me three times." Peter said, "Even if I must die with you, I will never disown you." But the words of Jesus proved to be true. Later that day Peter did deny knowing Jesus and when he heard a cock crow he remembered what Jesus had said and he wept bitterly. (Matthew 26: 75)

Peter was always learning from his master. He went with Jesus as they travelled from place to place. He listened and watched and he learnt more about God and the Kingdom of Heaven. When Jesus went back to heaven on Ascension Day, he told all his disciples to wait together for the gift of the Holy Spirit which he would send to them. After that they were to go into the world and teach the people and baptise them.

On the Day of Pentecost it was Peter who told the people gathered in Jerusalem the wonderful news of Jesus. On that day about three thousand new Christians were baptised. (Acts 2: 41) From that time on Peter and the other apostles continued their work for Jesus.

Prayers

1   Almighty God, who inspired your apostle St Peter to confess Jesus as Christ and Son of the living God, build up your church upon this rock, that in unity and peace it may proclaim one truth and follow one Lord, your son our Saviour Jesus Christ, who is alive and reigns with you and the Holy Spirit, one God, now and for ever. Amen.

2   Dear God, hear our praises. We thank you for Jesus who showed men how to be strong and kind. We thank you for Peter, who became strong to help those in trouble. Help us to be kind to everyone we meet and to do what we can to help them. Amen.

3   We thank you, O Lord, for your servants of old, who readily forsook all they had in answer to your call. Give us open ears to hear you speak and help us to be ready to obey your commands. May we, too, first learn from you and then teach others, both by our words and by our example, for the sake of Jesus Christ our Lord. Amen.

Hymns

When God made creation (WCV 119)
He lived for me, to show me (SM 35)

~ ~ ~ ~ ~ ~ ~ ~ ~ ~ ~ ~ ~

Q is for Quality
Gideon's Army

Sometimes you may hear people saying, "Quality is better than quantity." They mean that it is better to have a little of something good than a lot of something which is not so good.

Gideon was a true servant of God. God told Gideon that he would use him to give his people, Israel, victory over the Medianites and Amalekites. Gideon wondered how this could happen because the Medianites and Amalekites had a bigger army. But God gave Gideon all the signs he asked for to prove that it really was God himself who was speaking. As each of Gideon's prayers was answered, he became sure that God would be with him.

So he rose early one day and called all his people to him. (Judges 7: 1) The Lord spoke again to Gideon and said, "There are too many people with you. Tell the people that anyone who is frightened should leave at once and go back home." (Judges 7: 2–3) As Gideon made this announcement twenty-two thousand people left for home but still ten thousand remained. God knew it was better to have a few determined and courageous men than a great many who might prove cowardly or untrustworthy. When Gideon had gathered the remaining ten thousand men, God spoke to him again. He said, "There are still too many. Take them down to the water, and I will separate them. When I say to you, 'This man shall go with you', he shall go, and if I say, 'This man shall not go with you', he shall not go." (Judges 7: 4–5)

So Gideon ordered the men to go down to the water and God told him to choose for his army the men who drank water by cupping their hands and keeping watch all the time, as a dog does when it drinks. The men who knelt down by the water and drank straught from the stream, he was to turn away. Gideon sent away all the men who drank greedily, but the rest he kept with him. He now had an army of only three hundred men. However, these men had been carefully chosen. They were men of quality who would not let Gideon down. God ordered Gideon to attack the camp of the enemy straight away, and Gideon and his men defeated the Medianites and Amalekites. The quality of Gideon's army was more than equal to the large numbers in the armies of their enemies. Quality had proved better than quantity.

Prayers

1 O God our Father, may we try each day to give of our best in all that we do. May the work that we complete, the games that we play, the friends whom we choose, all improve the quality of our lives, which we offer to you. Amen.

2 O God, keep alive in our hearts that spirit of adventure which is not afraid to stand alone or to champion a difficult cause. May we follow those courageous people who in every age have fought for what is good. We ask this in the name of Jesus Christ our Lord. Amen.

3 O God, make us wise but do not let us be conceited,
Make us clear-sighted but do not let us be unkind,
Make us honest but do not let us be discourteous,
Make us strong-willed but do not let us be stubborn,
Make us to enjoy life but do not let us seek our pleasure only,
Make us pleasant to everyone, but do not let us lack sincerity. Amen.

Hymns

Fairest Lord Jesus (WCV 120)
I will bring you (CP 59)

~ ~ ~ ~ ~ ~ ~ ~ ~ ~ ~ ~ ~

Q is for the Queen of Sheba

The Queen visits Solomon

The Queen of Sheba was very wealthy and enjoyed showing off her splendour and magnificence. The Queen of Sheba heard about all the wonderful things that King Solomon possessed, so she decided to visit him to find out if the rumours she had heard were true. (1 Kings 10: 1–10)

So she set out for the court of King Solomon, taking with her great riches to impress this fine king. She wanted to find out not only how rich he was, but also if he was as wise as people said. She arrived in Jerusalem with many servants and with camels laden with spices, gold and precious stones. When she met King Solomon she asked him some very difficult questions. Solomon could answer them all and the queen was greatly impressed by his wisdom. She said to Solomon, "The stories about you and your wisdom are true, but I did not believe them until now."

They then exchanged gifts. The queen gave Solomon gold, spices and precious stones, and in exchange King Solomon gave the Queen of Sheba many rich gifts.

The legend of the waxen flowers

One of the tests the queen used to catch Solomon out was showing him some beautiful flowers. In every detail these flowers appeared real. Each fine marking was carefully imitated. But in fact the flowers were wax models.

The queen also showed him some similar flowers that were real. "I have heard much about your wisdom, sire," said the queen, "but I wish to put you to the test myself. You may not handle or smell either of these two bouquets of flowers, but I wish you to tell me which bouquet is made up of real blooms."

Solomon gazed at the two bunches of flowers. There was no way to tell the two apart. From every angle each petal on every flower seemed perfect, the veins on the leaves were perfectly formed, the stems of each bloom seemed identical. King Solomon seemed puzzled and the Queen of Sheba was certain the king would fail to answer. Solomon, however, did not hurry to make his judgement. He asked his servant to place the flowers on a table near the window and to open the window and let in some fresh air. Presently a bee flew in through the window. It buzzed round the waxen flowers, but did not settle. Very soon it passed on to the bouquet made up of the real blooms and settled down drawing nectar from the blossoms. "My little friend, the bee, has shown me the answer to your question, O Queen," said Solomon. "The flowers on which it has settled are of course the real ones."

And so Solomon proved again that his wisdom was beyond compare and the curiosity of the Queen of Sheba was satisfied.

Prayers

1   Lord give us strength upon the way,
And wisdom with each passing day,
That we may be both kind and true,
And do the best that we can do. Amen.

2   O Lord Jesus help us to be generous. May we always
be ready to share what we have with others, remembering that all good gifts come to us from you. Amen.

3   O Lord help us to trust in the judgement of others and
not always to have to test the good in others for
ourselves. Amen.

Hymns

Travel on, travel on (CP 42)
All the nations of the earth (CP 14)

~ ~ ~ ~ ~ ~ ~ ~ ~ ~ ~ ~ ~

Q is for Quietness

The Quakers and the Red Indians

There are times in every day, I'm sure, when you like a
few moments by yourself to be quiet and think things
over. You can think about what has happened or plan
what it is that you want to do next. When you are quiet
you can think about the right thing to do and decide about
things for yourself without being influenced by others.
The times when we are quiet are also times when we can
come close to God through prayer. Sometimes we worship
altogether, as in our morning assembly, or in church. But
our own prayers are most often spoken when we are
quietly on our own.

Members of the Society of Friends meet and keep
silence until some one in their group feels moved by God
to talk to the assembled people. These people are called
Quakers, and they never fight or go to war. They believe
that all differences of opinion must be settled in a peaceful
way.

Some of the early settlers in North America were
Quakers. A group of them had gathered one day for their
daily meeting of silent worship. It was hot inside the hut
and so they had left the door open, and all the grown-ups

148

and children were sitting quietly in the room. Nobody had felt called upon to speak and two of the very young children found it hard to concentrate their thoughts on God. Instead the two children began to gaze around them and to look longingly out of the window and through the door. They were surprised to see shadows moving outside and they nudged each other and began to feel uneasy. One of them wondered whether he should speak and warn the grown-ups of the feeling of danger he had. As he looked up he saw his grandfather looking at him. His grandfather showed him that he, too, knew about the movement outside, but there was nothing to fear. The two children trusted their grandfather and they stayed calm in the quietness of the room. Soon it became still again outside the hut. Whoever had been moving round spying on them had gone away.

But back in the forest, a young Red Indian boy was putting his arrow back into its quiver, with a puzzled expression on his face. "Why did you call me away, Father?" he asked the Red Indian Chieftain. "Why did you not allow me to shoot my arrow? I had an excellent aim." "My son," replied the Indian chief, "we do not need to make war upon these new settlers. I watched them as they sat together in their hut. They were waiting for the Great Spirit to speak to them, even as we watch and wait for his coming. Those people, I know, are peaceable people. They will do us no harm." Then his son understood. His father did not want him to destroy those who came to their land with kind thoughts and intentions. They feared only those white men who attacked them and would take their possessions from them. The peace and quietness of the Quakers' strong faith had kept them safe.

Let us ask that we may use all our quiet times to good advantage, so that we, too, may listen for the Great Spirit, who will always be our guide.

Prayers

1   Help us, O God, in a day which will be full of noise and bustle, to remember how Jesus spoke to you in the quietness of the wilderness. May we, too, seek you in the quietness, so that we may be aware of your Holy

Spirit, understand your will, and be filled with your peace. This we ask for Jesus Christ's sake. Amen.

2 O Lord Jesus Christ, we remember how your life was spent in the service of others, and how you found strength in periods of quietness and prayer. Make us ready to spend our lives in service; teach us how to find God in silence and how to pray. Then send us out to do your will, to the glory of your Holy Name. Amen.

3 O Lord Jesus, in the quiet of our hearts, speak to us day by day with your voice so gentle and so still. Teach us, O Lord, to have listening hearts, so that we may not miss the faintest whisper of your voice helping us to do what is right. Amen.

Hymns

Peace perfect peace (CP 53)
Kum ba yah my lord (CP 68)

~ ~ ~ ~ ~ ~ ~ ~ ~ ~ ~ ~ ~

R is for Reappearances
The great catch of fish

Jesus died on the cross on Good Friday and on Easter Day he rose from the dead. He had explained to the disciples, what was going to happen to him, but they were so sad when they buried Jesus in the tomb that they forgot what he had told them. However, it wasn't very long before their sorrow was turned to joy for they saw Jesus on Easter Day and then they knew, without doubt, that he had risen from the dead. Jesus remained on earth with his friends for forty days, from Easter Day until he went back to his father in heaven on Ascension Day. This time is called the Great Forty Days and during those days Jesus was seen by the disciples and others, and very quickly the news spread about the wonderful resurrection of Jesus. Everyone who saw Jesus believed what had happened and soon more and more people believed, too, even though they had not seen Jesus themselves.

On Easter Day the first person who saw Jesus was Mary Magdalene. That evening Jesus appeared to the disciples who were meeting together in the upper room. But there were other occasions when his friends saw him and each time Jesus came to them they were filled with joy.

One day some of the disciples had met beside the lake. Simon Peter said to them, "I am going out fishing." And the others all said, "We will go with you." (John 21: 3) They prepared the boat and set out. All night they spent fishing, but although they worked hard, they caught nothing.

When morning came they saw a man standing on the beach, who called out to them, "Friends, have you caught anything?" They replied, "No." The man said, "Cast your nets on the right side and you will make a good catch." The disciples did as they were told and they caught so many fish in their nets, they could not lift it into the boat. John realised at once that this miracle had happened because Jesus was there and he said to Peter, "It is the Lord." As soon as Peter heard that, he could not wait to get to Jesus. He jumped overboard and swam towards the beach. The other disciples followed in the boat, towing behind them the net full of fishes.

There was already a fire, with charcoal burning on it on

the beach. Some fish were cooking and there was bread also. Jesus said to them, "Bring some of your catch." Peter went aboard the fishing boat again and helped to drag in the net, which was heavy with the big fish they had caught. Jesus said to his friends, "Come and have breakfast." None of the disciples said to Jesus, "Who are you?", for they all knew that it was Jesus. Then Jesus took the bread and the fish and after blessing it, he gave it to his disciples to eat and they all had breakfast together on the shore.

The road to Emmaus

Another time Cleopas and a friend of his were walking to a village called Emmaus. (Luke 24: 13–35) As they walked they were talking about Jesus and all the sad things that had happened to him at the end of his life. Suddenly, a third person joined them. It was Jesus, but they did not know. Jesus asked them why they seemed so unhappy and upset. Cleopas said to him, "Are you the only person staying in Jerusalem who does not know what has happened there in the last few days?" Jesus said, "What do you mean?" And they answered that Jesus, their long awaited Messiah had been put to death on the cross and how they were feeling unhappy. They had heard that the women has found the tomb empty but they no longer knew what to believe.

Jesus continued to talk with them as they walked along, and yet the two friends did not realise who he was. When they reached Emmaus, they said to Jesus, "Come in and stay with us. The evening is closing in. It will soon be dark. You cannot continue your journey tonight." So Jesus went inside. They prepared a meal and Jesus sat down with them at the table. When they brought the bread, Jesus took it, broke it and blessed it. As soon as he did this, the two friends recognised him. They had been with him before when he had taken bread and blessed it and broken it and given it to his disciples to eat. As soon as the two disciples knew that it was Jesus, he disappeared from their sight again. But they said to each other, "Did we not feel our hearts on fire as he talked with us on the road and explained the scriptures to us?"

Then the two friends did not delay any longer. They set

out back to Jerusalem, so that they could tell the other disciples that they had seen Jesus and all that had taken place as they walked along the road to Emmaus.

Prayers

1   Almighty Father, who in your great mercy made glad the disciples with the sight of the risen Lord, give us such knowledge of his presence with us, that we may be strengthened and sustained by his risen life and serve you continually in righteousness and truth, through Jesus Christ our Lord. Amen.

2   Dear Lord Jesus, you comforted your sorrowing friends when you reappeared after you had risen from the dead. Help us to share the joy that the disciples felt at that time, as we try our best to serve you day by day. Amen.

3   All praise be yours, O risen Lord,
    From death to endless life restored.
    All praise to God the Father be
    And Holy Spirit eternally. Amen.

Hymns

Sing life, sing love, sing Jesus (SM 29)
Haul, haul away (SM 58)

~ ~ ~ ~ ~ ~ ~ ~ ~ ~ ~ ~ ~

R is for Reassurance

The resurrection

When we have to decide for ourselves what to do or sometimes when things are difficult, we ask someone's advice, so that we can feel reassured. When we know that we are acting in the right way, then we again feel confident to continue as we had started. Everyone needs reassurance from time to time, grown-ups as well as children.

There are times when, even if we believe something with all our hearts, we like someone to tell us again that our belief is true. It gives us the reassurance we need. After the disciples had seen Jesus die on the cross, they needed a lot of reassurance before they could fully understand the wonderful events of Easter Day. Jesus understood how his friends were feeling and he reappeared before them many times before he went back to his father in heaven on Ascension Day. When he left his friends on earth, he promised them he would not be leaving them alone. He said he would send them his Holy Spirit to be with them and to guide them as they set out to spread the news of God's kingdom to all parts of the world. The very last words he spoke to his disciples were these, "And be assured, I am with you always, to the end of time." (Matthew 28: 20)

Doubting Thomas

One of the disciples who needed the greatest amount of reassurance was Thomas. (John 20: 24–29) He had not been with the rest of the disciples on Easter Day evening when Jesus had come to them in the upper room. They were all anxious to tell Thomas what had happened and they eagerly described the events. "We have seen the Lord," they told Thomas. But Thomas could not believe in such a miracle. He thought the disciples were making up the story to give themselves comfort. He felt no reassurance as he listened to his friends. He said, "Unless I see the mark of the nails on his hands, unless I put my finger into the place where the nails were, and my hand into his side, I will not believe it." A week later, when Thomas was with the other disciples, Jesus came to them again saying, "Peace be with you!" Then he said to Thomas, "Reach your hand here and put it into my side. Be unbelieving no longer, but believe." From that moment, all Thomas's doubts vanished and he too knew the gladness and joy that the other disciples had.

We often seek reassurance. When we are troubled we can pray. God will always listen. He is always there to comfort us and reassure us, and he will remain with us throughout our lives. With this reassurance we know that we have nothing to fear.

Prayers

1   Dear Lord Jesus, you have given us the assurance that we are never alone, for you are always by our side.

Help us always to trust you, to love you and to serve you, that we may be worthy of you in all that we do. Amen.

2 O Lord Jesus, you are our friend. Help us to treat our friends with the same consideration as you showed for others. May we always comfort, reassure and help our friends and those we love, and in this way we know that we shall be pleasing you. Amen.

3 O Spirit of the living Christ, come to us and fill our lives with your joy and power. We rejoice that you conquered death and that you came back to your friends full of life and love. Give us, we pray, the reassurance that you are with us always, and that you can give us the strength to do right and the power to work for you. Teach us to be cheerful and happy-hearted, good companions to old and young. Amen.

Hymns

There's not a tint that paints the rose (WCV 85)
Can you be sure that the rain will fall (CP 34)

~ ~ ~ ~ ~ ~ ~ ~ ~ ~ ~ ~ ~

R is for Rock

St Peter

The first thing anyone has to do if he wants to build a house, is to test the ground it will stand on. If the ground is too wet or marshy, or too dry and sandy, special construction work has to go into the foundations to make the house safe. Every house has to be built on good foundations. If all the preparation work is not done thoroughly the building will fall down.

The parable of the house on the rock

Jesus told a story about building on firm foundations. He had been teaching the people and now he wanted them to understand that they must act upon his teaching if it was to have any real effect on their lives. He said, "What then of the man who hears these words of mine and acts upon them? He is like a man who had the sense to build his house on rock. The rain came down, the floods rose, the

155

wind blew, and beat upon that house, but it did not fall, because its foundations were on rock. But what of the man who hears these words of mine and does not act upon them? He is like a man who was foolish enough to build his house on sand. The rain came down, the floods rose, the wind blew, and beat upon that house and down it fell with a great crash." (Matthew 7: 24–27)

One of the disciples, was called Simon. Jesus gave him a new name, Peter, which meant a rock. Jesus knew that although there were times when Peter might do things he would regret, yet he was a strong man with a firm faith. Jesus knew that in the end Peter would not let him down. He knew that Peter was building up a very good foundation through listening to his teaching and doing his best to act on it. One day Jesus asked his disciples who the people thought he was. They gave him many different answers. They said that some thought he was John the Baptist, others that he was Elijah or Jeremiah or another of the prophets. Jesus then turned to Peter and said, "Who do you say I am?" Simon answered without hesitation, "You are the Messiah, the Son of the living God." Then Jesus knew that Simon had come to know him through his heavenly Father and he said, "And I say this to you. You are Peter, the rock, and on this rock I will build my church." (Matthew 16: 18)

Jesus knew Peter would stand up to all the storms and difficulties of the years ahead. Peter was well named the rock. He carried on the work when Jesus went back to his Father in heaven and he was one of the apostles who spread the good news of Jesus into all the world. Peter became a rock on which the church was built.

Let us try to make our foundations so strong that whatever we build on them will stand firm no matter how much the rains may beat down or the winds blow.

Prayers

1   O Lord Jesus Christ, you have taught us that we should build the foundation of our lives upon solid rock. Help us to seek the things that will enable us to achieve this. May we use all the talents God has given us, do our work well and with pleasure, offer our help to others, and always try to serve you. Amen.

2 Almighty God, we do not know what the future holds for us but we do know that it will provide many opportunities for service to others. Help us to prepare ourselves so that when such opportunities arise we may be found ready and willing to give of our best, in the name of Jesus Christ, our Lord. Amen.

3 Christ is our corner-stone,
On him alone we build,
With his true saints alone
The courts of heaven are filled:
On his great love
Our hopes we place
Of present grace
And joys above. Amen.

Hymns

All over the world everywhere (CP 61)
My faith it is an oaken staff (CP 46)

~ ~ ~ ~ ~ ~ ~ ~ ~ ~ ~ ~ ~

S is for Saints
St Stephen

People who have spent their lives serving God and helping people are sometimes made saints. Stephen was a strong and fearless Christian. Jesus had promised to send his Holy Spirit to the disciples, and they waited together in Jerusalem until this happened. When they were filled with the power of the Holy Spirit they set out to spread the faith to as many people as they could reach. The disciples had so much to do that they needed more people to work with them and so they chose seven more helpers. Stephen was among them.

There were many people who did not agree with all that Stephen said and they came forward and argued with him. But Stephen could answer all their arguments. He believed with his whole heart that what he was teaching the people was the truth about God and about his son, Jesus Christ. At last, his enemies took hold of Stephen and made him stand trial before the council. They accused him falsely but Stephen was unafraid, and as all those who were sitting in the council fixed their eyes upon him, Stephen looked straight back at them. The high priest asked Stephen if what his accusers said about him was true, and Stephen replied by begging the members of the council to listen to him.

What he said made the members of the council very angry. But Stephen looked up to heaven and saw Jesus standing at God's right hand. "Look," he said, "there is a rift in the sky; I can see the Son of Man standing at God's right hand." (Acts 7: 55–57) Then his enemies were furious, for they had not seen the vision. They shouted at Stephen and blocked their ears, so that they could not hear anything more that he said. They rushed at Stephen and flung him outside. They chased him away from the city and then they started stoning him. Those who were watching took off their coats and they gave them to Saul to look after. Then they, too, picked up stones and began to hurl them at Stephen. Stephen could not defend himself against the attack of such a wild mob. He knew that these angry people would soon kill him and he prayed out loud, saying, "Lord Jesus, receive my spirit." As he fell to the ground, he called loudly to God saying, "Lord, do not hold this sin against them." (Acts 7: 60) As he finished his prayer, Stephen died. He was murdered by those who would not listen to him and Saul, who later became St Paul, was among those who watched Stephen die.

So Stephen became the first Christian martyr, having died for his faith. Today many churches bear his name, because Christians are proud to remember the good and brave life of St Stephen. Stephen's special day is very close to Christmas, on 26 December, the day we most often call Boxing Day. You can probably remember this date easily if you recall the words of the carol that begins "Good King Wenceslas looked out, On the feast of Stephen." When you next sing that carol, you can think about St Stephen and how courageous he was in the hands of his enemies.

Prayers

1 Heavenly Father, give us grace, in all our sufferings for the truth, to follow the example of your first martyr Saint Stephen; that we also may look to him who was crucified and pray for those who persecute us; through Jesus Christ our Lord. Amen.

2 For your dear saints, O Lord,
   Who strove like you to live,
   Who followed you, obeyed, adored,
   Our grateful prayers receive. Amen.

3 O God of saints, to you we pray,
   O Saviour, be with us each day,
   O Holy Spirit, guide and friend
   Grant us your grace, till life shall end,
   That with all saints our rest may be
   In heaven, with them, all praising thee. Amen.

Hymns

For all the saints (WCV 12)
Ye holy angels bright (WCV 21)

~ ~ ~ ~ ~ ~ ~ ~ ~ ~ ~ ~

S is for Samson
Samson and Delilah

The Philistines were very strong, and they ruled over the Israelites for forty years. Among the Israelites there was a good man called Manoah. One day an angel of the Lord visited his wife and promised her that she should have a son. The angel said that she must live a pure life and when her son was born, she was not to shave or cut his hair. The angel promised that her son had been chosen by God to help the Israelites free themselves from the Philistines. (Judges 13: 2–6) In due course Manoah's wife gave birth to a son and called him Samson.

When he was a young man, Samson had extraordinary strength. Samson believed that this special power came to him through his hair. Before he had been born, his mother had been told by the angel never to cut his hair, and it had grown very long. Samson was very proud of his hair, and he was proud, too, of his great strength. Samson fell in love with a woman called Delilah. She was a Philistine and God had a plan for Samson and Delilah. God had promised that Samson should help save the Israelites from the Philistines and so he brought Samson and Delilah together. Delilah begged Samson to tell her his secret. She wanted to know where his great strength came from. Samson had never told anyone that he believed his strength lay in his hair. At first he gave Delilah other reasons for his power, but she knew he was not telling her the truth. At last Samson grew weary of her nagging at him and he said, "No razor has ever touched my head. If my head were shaved, then my strength would leave me, and I should become as weak as any other man."

Once Delilah knew Samson's secret, she went at once to the Philistines and she said, "Come at once, he has told me his secret." Delilah lulled Samson to sleep, and whilst he slept a man was called to shave off Samson's hair. When Delilah saw that nearly all Samson's hair had been cut off, she called out to him, "The Philistines are upon you, Samson." Then Samson woke up, but all his great strength had left him. He was weak and helpless, surrounded by his enemies. Then the Philistines bound him in chains. They took him to prison and they blinded him.

The Philistines rejoiced that Samson was now in their hands. He was the one Israelite whom they feared. But whilst he was a prisoner, Samson's hair gradually began to grow again and little by little he felt his strength returning to him. When the Philistines were having a great party one day they all became very merry. (Judges 17: 25) They shouted, "Call Samson, and let him fight to make sport for us." They wanted to mock Samson whilst he was blind and too weak to defend himself. So Samson was brought into the court where all the leaders of the Philistines had gathered. He asked the boy who brought him in to lead him to the pillars so that he could feel them and lean against them, as he could not see his way. Samson felt the pillars on each side of him with his hands. Then Samson called on the Lord God and prayed with all his heart, "Remember me, O Lord God," he called out, "Give me strength only this once, O God, and let me at one stroke be avenged on the Philistines for my two eyes." (Judges 17: 28) Then Samson put his arms round the two central pillars that supported the temple, braced himself and said, "Let me die with the Philistines." He leaned forward with all his might, and the temple fell on the people who were in it.

Samson died with the Philistines that day. But by his death, he delivered his people from the power of the Philistines as God had promised he would.

Prayers

1 O Lord God, we thank you for our health and strength. Help us always to use our growing strength to help others and those in need. May we use all our good gifts to your glory. Amen.

2 For all the strength we have,
To run and leap and play,
For all our limbs so sound and strong,
We bring our thanks today. Amen.

3 May the strength of god pilot us,
May the power of God preserve us,
May the wisdom of God instruct us,
May the hand of God protect us,
Now and for evermore. Amen.

161

Hymns

Spirit of God as strong as the wind (CP 63)
Now in the days of youth (WCV 65)

~ ~ ~ ~ ~ ~ ~ ~ ~ ~ ~ ~

S is for Service

The life of Albert Schweitzer

About twenty years ago a very well known and much loved person died. He had a name that started with "S" and he became famous in his own lifetime, which he dedicated to the service of others. He was Dr Albert Schweitzer and he was an old man of ninety when he died.

When he was a young man, Schweitzer used all his opportunities to learn as much as he could. He promised himself that he would work at his own studies until he was thirty years old, and then for the rest of his life, he would serve and help those who needed him most. Schweitzer was very gifted and he enjoyed music. He learned to play the organ and he composed music. He became a famous musician. Schweitzer read many books and also wrote books himself. He liked to gather crowds of people together and talk to them about the love of Jesus. He liked to talk, too, about his chosen work.

But all this was not enough to satisfy Schweitzer. He felt sure in his heart that God wanted him to go to Africa. There were many poor, sick and starving people there with no one to care about them and help them lead better lives. More than anything else these people needed a doctor. So Schweitzer studied medicine as well. He trained and qualified as a doctor and he set out to serve a particular community in Africa. He took with him the medical supplies he knew he would need, and he also took his piano, which he loved.

Until Schweitzer arrived at the mission station of Lambarene in Africa, the native people had only been able to turn to the witch doctors for help. Nothing had been prepared for Dr Schweitzer's arrival. There was a small bungalow for him to move into, but there was no hospital, there were no nurses, there were no supplies. The people were scattered over a large area. However, once the word spread round that a doctor had arrived at Lambarene, the people came from far and near to get the help they so desperately needed. Some of the local people helped Dr Schweitzer to clean out an old chicken-house and turn it into a hospital. Here the doctor carried out much of his work with only an old camp bed for an operating table. All day he treated his patients. He also supervised the construction of more buildings so that he could treat more sick people. Late into the night, Albert Schweitzer played his piano, wrote more books and sent reports of his work back to Europe. No matter how hard or how late he worked, he was always up early and ready for his first patients the following day. On Sundays, he did only the work that was essential in his hospital and then he held services for the African people, to teach them about the love of Jesus. Dr Schweitzer would play the hymns at the services and always he spoke to the people as well.

When war broke out Dr Schweitzer had to leave Africa for a time. The people there had come to love him and were sad to see him go. But Dr Schweitzer knew that one day he would return, because God had called him to work among the African people. Whilst he was away, Dr Schweitzer gave many concerts to raise money for his missionary work at Lambarene. He was also a popular speaker. On his return to Africa he used the money to clear a large area of the jungle where he built a hospital with more facilities and better equipment.

When Schweitzer returned home for visits, he was welcomed as a hero and many people gave him gifts to help him with his work. He was awarded the Nobel Peace Prize and he used the money to build a special village to house 300 people who suffered from leprosy. One of the helpers at Lambarene who worked with Dr Schweitzer wrote this about their new home, "We live and work in trust and confidence. When necessary, doctors and nurses work day and night without thinking about time. The patients have freedom throughout the hospital. They fish in the river, they take their firewood from the forest, they eat all they want of the fruits which are grown. Everything is free for them. The children are playing everywhere. The animals know they can live in security here. They are not killed for food."

By the time Albert Schweitzer reached the end of his life, over a thousand people were being housed and fed at the hospital every day. Among the Africans, there were six more doctors and thirty-five nurses at work and still more buildings were being planned to care for more patients. How different Lambarene must have looked then from the deserted, dirty, uncared-for site which had greeted Dr Schweitzer on his first day at the African mission station. When Dr Schweitzer died, a learned professor said of him, "In all humility let us salute a faithful soldier of Christ, seeing in him an example of Christian service long to be remembered."

Prayers

1   O God, we ask for your blessing on all missionaries and other devoted people who give their lives to the service of others in foreign lands. May their courage never fail and may they know that they are supported by our prayers in their work for you. Amen.

2   Heavenly Father, as we come before you, we would dedicate to your service all that we have and are. We also bring to you all that we hope to be. Help us to offer ourselves to you, and go with us all, guiding and guarding our steps as we travel on the way. Amen.

3   Tell me, why are there people around me
Hungry and needy and lonely and sad?
The world must be mad.
Why can't we give
So that others may live.

Tell me, something that I could do,
Something that would be positive,
Useful and kind,
Oh help me to find,
Some way to serve mankind. Amen.

Hymns

God my father, loving me (WCV 46)
Remember all the people (WCV 70)

~ ~ ~ ~ ~ ~ ~ ~ ~ ~ ~ ~

S is for Shepherd
The parable of the hundred sheep

When Jesus was alive there were many shepherds in the countryside in Palestine and people were used to seeing them and knew a lot about their work. A good shepherd led a hard and busy life. He knew each of his sheep and he cared for every one and would watch over them all to keep them safe.

Jesus told a very well known parable about a shepherd who had a hundred sheep. (Matthew 18: 12–14) One night when the shepherd was counting his sheep he discovered that he had only ninety-nine. The shepherd made sure his flock would be watched over by the other shepherds, and then he went back to all the places he had been to with his sheep that day. He had walked many miles in search of good pasture land and now it was late at night and the shepherd must have felt tired. But he thought only about the sheep that was lost, which might be hurt. As the shepherd searched he called out from time to time, so that if the sheep was near it would hear and recognise his voice and give an answering bleat. At last he discovered his lost sheep and carried it back to the fold. When the shepherds saw him returning with the lost sheep they shared his joy and rejoiced with him. All his sheep were safe again. The lost one was back among the others and the flock was complete.

And Jesus explained that God, our heavenly Father, is also full of joy when we are safely in his care. If we do wrong and stray from the rest of the flock he looks for us and welcomes us back when we are sorry and ask to be forgiven. God's love and care surrounds us all the time, just as the shepherd watches constantly over his sheep. Jesus said, "I am the good shepherd."

Prayers

1   O Lord Jesus, you are the great shepherd of the sheep, help us to walk in your footsteps day by day. Give us grace to follow where you lead, so that we may be enfolded in the love of your flock for ever. Amen.

2   The king of love my shepherd is,
    Whose goodness faileth never;
    I nothing lack if I am his
    And he is mine for ever.

    Perverse and foolish oft I strayed,
    But yet in love he sought me,
    And on his shoulder gently laid,
    And home rejoicing brought me. Amen.

3   Dear Lord Jesus, we know that you will love and care
    for us at all times. Thank you for being our loving
    Father and the good shepherd to all people in every
    part of the world. Amen.

Hymns

Loving shepherd of thy sheep (WCV 35)
The king of love my shepherd is (WCV 37)

~ ~ ~ ~ ~ ~ ~ ~ ~ ~ ~ ~ ~

S is for Sikh

The legend of the name Singh

When Sikh children are baptised every boy and girl has a
special name given to him or to her. Each boy has the
name Singh as his second name. The word *Singh* means
lion. Every girl is given the name Kaur, which means
princess. Apart from that there are no special names for
boys or for girls. The names suit either sex, just as we call
boys or girls Francis or Lee, or Vivian.

Sikhs have other customs that seem strange to us but
which are part of their religious life. Sikhs do not cut their
hair but they cover it with a turban. They wear steel
bracelets on their right arms to remind them of God and
that they must do no wrong with their hands. Their
religion tells them, too, that they must work hard, worship God and live unselfishly. The Sikhs follow the
teachings of the ten great Gurus, who were their leaders
and who explained to them how they must behave. Sikhs
recite part of their sacred scriptures three times a day.
They work hard to earn their own living. They do not
expect others to carry their responsibilities for them, but
they give part of the money they earn to support the old,
the sick and the handicapped. Because boys have the

name Singh they are expected to be very brave, as brave as lions. Many Sikhs have chosen to be soldiers and have fought bravely in the army. They are loyal men with a strong sense of duty.

This story tells how all Sikh boys came to be given the name of Singh. In a Sikh Temple, the Holy Book is guarded by five armed men. Long ago the Guru had to choose some men to guard the scriptures. He wanted men who would be fearless in their duty, no matter what dangers they encountered. He had to think of a way to make sure that only the bravest men offered to be guards. So the Guru stood outside his temple and he called to the people saying, "Who among you is brave enough to risk having his head cut off and will guard our Holy Book in the temple?"

For a while no one spoke, but then one man said, "I will, for I do not know of a more honourable way to die." He went inside the temple but he was not seen again. Then the Guru once more stood before the people. His sword was dripping with blood as he said, "Is there a second man prepared to step forward?" A second man volunteered and he was followed by another and another and another, until five men had gone from the crowd. Eventually the Guru came outside the temple again and this time he seemed well pleased. "The men who followed me into the temple," he said, "were as brave as lions. From this day they shall be called Singh and all will remember that they were prepared, if necessary, to die in the cause of their duty." The five guards then came out. None of them had actually been harmed.

Since that time all the men and boys of the Sikh faith have tried to follow bravely in the steps of the ten great Gurus, and they bear the name of Singh with pride.

Prayers

1   O God our Father, help us to be as brave as lions as we go about our work each day. May we try to work as hard as we can and to be of service to others in all our actions. Amen.

2   Help us, O God, to find time each day to remember you. When we pray, may we listen for your voice telling us what we should do. May we study your word and understand your will. Help us to open our hearts and to let you in. Amen.

3   Teach us, good Lord, to use our gifts in the service of others. Make our feet willing, our hands useful, our minds active and our hearts pure in your service, for Jesus Christ's sake. Amen.

Hymns

Think, think on these things (SM 1)
All things praise thee, Lord most high (WCV 9)

~ ~ ~ ~ ~ ~ ~ ~ ~ ~ ~ ~

T is for Talents
The parable of the bags of gold

God has given us life. He has made us and he has given special gifts and talents to each one of us. Our special talents are meant to be used and shared and given back to God for his glory. It is always sad to see people who do not use their skills to advantage or who are too lazy to improve their natural ability.

Jesus told a parable to explain how God wants each person to make full use of the talents he or she has been given. The parable also explains how talents increase if they are used as God intended they should be. (Matthew 25: 14–28) The story Jesus told was about a man who had three servants. One day the master called his servants together, and he told them that he had to go abroad for a time. Whilst he was away, he wanted his servants to take care of his property for him. He knew his servants had different experience and capabilities. Some had been with him longer than the others. So the master said to his most senior servant, "Here are five bags of gold. Take care of these whilst I am gone." To the next servant the master gave two bags of gold and the third one received one bag only. The gold was not a present. It was the master's money and he was leaving it with his servants so that they should put it to good use while he was gone.

The first servant took his five bags of gold. He thought carefully about how to use the money. He did not waste the money or spend it foolishly, but he went into business and worked hard and soon he was making a profit. The second servant, who had two bags of gold, did very much the same. He also invested the money wisely. However, the third servant was afraid. He had the chance to take his bag of gold and put it to good use, but he did not have the courage to try. He decided the best thing he could do was to keep the gold just as it was. So he dug a hole in the ground and he hid his master's money. Consequently all the time his master was away he failed to do anything useful with his time or the money.

A long time afterwards the master returned from his visit abroad. He called his servants together to see what they had done with the bags of gold he had given them and to reward them accordingly. The first servant came forward eagerly, "Master," he said, "you left five bags with me. I have made five more." "Well done, my good servant!" said the master. "You have proved trustworthy in something small. I will now put you in charge of something big. Come and share your master's delight." Then it was the turn of the servant who had been left with two bags of gold. He came forward and he said, "Master, you left two bags with me. I have made two more." "Well done my good servant!" said the master. "You have proved trustworthy in something small. I will now put you in charge of something big. Come and share your master's delight."

The third servant then had to come before the master and say what had happened to his bag of gold. He had nothing to show for the time and the opportunities he had wasted. He tried to make excuses. "Master," he said, "I thought you were a hard man. I was afraid of losing your money and so I did not use it wisely. But it is safe. I went and hid your money in the ground. Here it is. I give you back what belongs to you." Then the master was angry. He was angry with his servant because he had been lazy and refused to use the talents he had been given. If he had tried and failed, his master would probably have praised his efforts, but he had done nothing except shrink away from the chances he had been given. "You are a lazy rascal," said the master. "Now I'll take from you the gold you had and give it to my servant who has worked hardest and used his talents best."

Let us make sure that we use all our talents. The older we grow the more and more opportunities we have to use them for our own good and to help other people. In this way we shall give of our best and our lives will be enriched as a result.

Prayers

1   Dear Lord Jesus, you have made our lives rich with all the skills and talents you have given to us. Help us to use all our opportunities wisely so that we may increase our talents and give back into your service the good gifts we have received from you. Amen.

Talent : a special ability.

2　Give us, O Lord, a steadfast will
　　To meet whatever there may be.
　　To face the future unafraid
　　With courage and serenity.
　　Give us, O Lord, a heart at peace
　　Our strength sustain, our faith increase. Amen.

3　O God,
　　Help us to offer our minds to you, that we may always
　　be guided by you.
　　Help us to offer our tongues to you, that we may bring
　　comfort to those who are sad.
　　Help us to offer our hand to you, that we may help
　　those who are in need.
　　Help us to offer our feet to you, that we may carry the
　　good news of Jesus into the dark corners of this life.
　　Help us, O God, to offer back to you the lives you gave
　　us, more fulfilled and more enriched.
　　We ask this in the name of Jesus Christ Our Lord.
　　Amen.

Hymns

Lord of all good, our gifts we bring to thee (100 HT 60)
The wise may bring their learning (WCV 48)

~ ~ ~ ~ ~ ~ ~ ~ ~ ~ ~ ~

T is for Thanks

Jesus and the ten lepers

Saying "thank you" is a very simple thing to do and yet it
is amazing how quickly and easily some people forget to
do it. Jesus noticed when people remembered to say thank
you. He was pleased with those who did and he was
saddened by those who forgot, who did now show that
they appreciated the help they had received. We can read
in St Luke's Gospel of ten lepers who came to Jesus. (Luke
17: 11–19)

　One day Jesus was on his way to Jerusalem and had to
pass through a village. As he approached the village, ten
lepers came towards him. The men knew they mustn't
come too close to Jesus, so they stood some distance away
and shouted, "Jesus, Master, take pity on us." When Jesus
saw the lepers he said to them, "Go and show yourselves

171

to the priests." Anyone who believed he had been cured of leprosy had to go to the priest, and the priest would decide if he really was free of the disease. The ten men set off immediately, and on their way, their leprosy left them. Jesus had worked a great miracle for each of the sick men. All ten were well again and could return to their homes and families.

How full of joy they must have felt. Moments before they had nothing to look forward to, except a worsening of their illness and eventual death. Suddenly all this was changed. Their bodies had been made whole again.

One of the ten, when he found that he was cured, turned back praising God aloud. He threw himself down at Jesus' feet and thanked him. Jesus looked at him and said, "Were not all ten cleansed? The other nine, where are they? Why haven't they come back to give praise to God?" Jesus must have felt saddened by the ingratitude of the nine thoughtless men.

Let us make sure that we don't cause sadness to others by forgetting to show our thanks for all the blessings we receive. And above all, let us remember every day to give thanks to God for all his goodness to us.

Prayers

1   Whether we mutter a thank you or not,
    We're most of us glad for what we have got;
    So let us today, and all through the year,
    Thank God with words that are joyful to hear. Amen.

2   Give us always thankful hearts, O Lord, for all your goodness and loving kindness to us, above all for your love in sending Jesus Christ our Lord to be the saviour of the world. Help us to remember that everything we have comes to us from you, so that our hearts may always be thankful and that we may praise you, not only with our lips, but in our lives, by giving ourselves to your service, and by walking with you day by day. Through Jesus Christ our Lord. Amen.

3   Dear Father God, thank you for loving and caring for us every day of our lives. Help us to remember your love, and to love you in return. Amen.

4   Father we thank you for the night
     And for the pleasant morning light,
     For rest, and food, and loving care,
     And all that makes the day so fair. Amen.

Hymns

Now thank we all our God (WCV 25)
Autumn days when the glass is jewelled (CP 4)

~ ~ ~ ~ ~ ~ ~ ~ ~ ~ ~ ~ ~

T is for Trust

Blondin the tight-rope walker

There was once a very famous Frenchman called Blondin, who was a tight-rope walker. One of his greatest acts was to cross the Niagara Falls on a tight-rope. If he had slipped, he would certainly have been killed. However, he had complete confidence in his own ability. He stepped on to the tight-rope, holding a balancing rod and walked across. Then to the amazement of the crowd, he crossed back again pushing a wheelbarrow. The people held their breath, hardly daring to watch this remarkable man. They wanted to see every step, yet they were afraid that he would fall. When he was safely back, the crowd clapped and shouted their applause and appreciation. One man in the crowd kept shouting, "Do it again! Do it again!" Blondin searched for the man and said to him, "Do you really believe I can do it again?" "Of course, I do," replied the man, "I've seen you do it once. I know you can do it again." "Very well," answered Blondin, "You climb into my wheelbarrow and I will push you across." The man was quickly silenced. He believed Blondin could perform this feat, but he did not trust him with his life! His belief in Blondin lacked complete faith.

St Paul is shipwrecked

St Paul, on the other hand, showed perfect trust in God when he was faced with great danger. He had been taken prisoner and he and others had to leave by sea. He knew that the weather was too rough for the ship to put to sea safely and he advised the captain not to leave until the storm had passed. The captain would not listen to Paul and so he and the other prisoners were taken on board with the centurions and other passengers. At first the voyage went more smoothly than expected, but gradually the weather worsened. Before long the captain had to lighten the weight of the ship by throwing things overboard.

When the storm was still at its worst, St Paul stood up among the crew and passengers and told them that an angel of God had told him that they would all be safe. After fourteen more nights, they saw land. They tried to take the ship ashore, but it got caught in the currents and ran aground. Paul gave orders that everyone who could swim should jump overboard and get to land first. They then helped the others to leave the ship and they all came safely to land.

Paul had trusted in God and his faith had helped all the other people on the voyage to reach land safely. Many of the people who had been with Paul were so amazed by his great faith that they became Christians.

Prayers

1 Lord Jesus Christ, we know that you are always with us. Help us to trust in you with all our hearts. Increase our faith and let us follow in your footsteps day by day. Amen.

2 O loving Father of us all,
Who by your power has set us free.
O may we answer to your call,
And evermore to trust in thee.
There's nothing more we need to ask,
But faith to follow you until
We're overcome and done the task
That's set, because it is your will. Amen.

3 I hear no voice, I feel no touch,
I see no glory bright;
But yet I know that God is near,
In darkness as in light.

He watches ever by my side,
And hears my whispered prayer;
The Father for his little child
Both day and night does care. Amen.

4   Courage, brother, do not stumble,
    Though the path be dark as night
    There's a star to guide the humble,
    Trust in God and do the right. Amen.

Hymns

God who has made the earth (WCV 83)
Praise him in the morning (CP 40)

~ ~ ~ ~ ~ ~ ~ ~ ~ ~ ~ ~

T is for Truth

The boy who cried "Wolf"

One of the worst things about telling lies is that people stop believing us. The moment comes when we do speak truthfully but no one trusts us any more. You may have heard before about the boy who cried wolf. Hans was a shepherd boy. He was quite young when he first had to go on his own up into the hills to take care of the sheep. His uncle promised him that if he was in danger, everyone in the village would come to help him he if called for help.

Hans was proud of himself as he began his work. He felt grown up and important. For a few days all was well. But then Hans began to get bored, watching the sheep all day. There was nothing much to do and it was a lonely occupation. Hans decided to play a little trick on the villagers. When all was peaceful in the afternoon, Hans suddenly ran down the hillside. He waved his arms and shouted, "Wolf, wolf." The villagers heard Hans's cries. They grabbed what sticks and weapons they could and hurried up the hillside to help Hans and save the sheep. But when they arrived, breathless, to where the sheep were grazing, they found that all was peaceful. They realised what Hans had been up to and they were angry. Hans thought it all a good joke. He was pleased with himself and thought he had been very clever.

Some days passed peacefully and then Hans wanted a bit more fun. His little trick had worked very well before. It had brought everyone running and had provided a splendid afternoon's entertainment for him, and so Hans decided to repeat his game. When all was quiet in the early afternoon, down the hillside he ran again, shouting, "Wolf, wolf," at the top of his voice. The faithful villagers

175

again rushed to help the young shepherd boy. Each one hurried up the hillside to see what he could do to help. Hans had a good laugh at their expense. The villagers, though, were angry that their time had again been wasted.

All was quiet again for the next few days. Then, one peaceful afternoon, a wolf really did wander over the hillside. It saw the grazing flock and at once leapt in to attack. It killed the first sheep, and the rest of the flock scattered in terror, bleating piteously. Hans was horrified. He ran down the hillside for help, desperately calling out, "Wolf, wolf". The villagers heard him but each and everyone of them went on with his own work. "It's only Hans," they said, "up to his usual tricks again." Hans tried to explain that this time he really was telling the truth. No one believed him. No one trusted him any more. Hans found out the hard way that his lack of truthfulness had led to his own downfall.

Prayers

1   May all the words we speak today
    Be honest, brave and true,
    O God, our Father, help us be
    Obedient unto you. Amen.

2   Dear Lord Jesus, help us always to be honest in the way we behave. Guard our lips from telling lies. Make us trustworthy and responsible; for Jesus' sake. Amen.

3   It was such a little lie,
    Saying "No" instead of "Yes",
    Yet it spoiled the glad new day
    Father God had meant to bless.

    For this horrid little lie
    Told so quickly, lasted long;
    Dimmed the shining truth of God
    And made everything seem wrong.

    There was only one way out,
    But it was a happy way:
    "Father God, forgive your child,"
    Were the words I had to say. Amen.

Hymns

In our work and in our play (WCV 32)
Can it be true, the things they say of you (SM 37)

~ ~ ~ ~ ~ ~ ~ ~ ~ ~ ~ ~ ~

U is for Ugliness
The ugly duckling

Hans Andersen wrote a story about an ugly duckling. From the very beginning, his life was miserable. All the animals in the farmyard, even his own family, disliked him because he was ugly. He was pecked and chased and teased, until he decided to leave the farmyard altogether.

Even this did not solve his problems. The outside world was no kinder to him and the poor little duckling had a hard job to survive the cold weather of the winter months. Many times he came close to death and he was so unhappy that he wanted to die. But the winter passed and when the warmer days of spring came the ugly duckling began to feel stronger and braver. He left the lonely pond where he had lived during the winter and began to swim down the river. On the river the ugly duckling saw three white swans being fed by children. The ugly duckling thought they were the most beautiful birds he had ever seen. As the three swans swam towards him he hung his head ashamed of his own ugliness. He thought the swans would attack him. He had been attacked often. Now he felt ready to die, so he did not try to move away.

The children on the river bank were calling out excitedly that they had seen a fourth swan on the river. The ugly duckling looked round to see this bird and found himself surrounded by the other swans who were greeting him with pleasure. They were accepting him as one of them- selves. The ugly duckling could hardly believe it. He looked down into the water and there was his reflection. He was not yet fully grown, but there was no doubt at all that he had become a swan. All the miseries of the past were quickly forgotten, and the beautiful young swan sailed down the river with his three new companions.

Nobody ever wants to be like the ugly duckling. We all want to be attractive in our own way and liked by friends and people we meet. Although there are many things about ourselves that we cannot change, we never have to appear ugly. Nobody is ugly when his or her face is lit up by a smile. Nobody is ugly when his or her eyes sparkle with interest. Nobody is ugly whose hands are always busily looking to see where they can help. Nobody is ugly if his or her heart is full of love and kindness, because this shows in the expression on that person's face. And if we always look for the good and not the faults in others, then we shall see what is beautiful.

Prayers

1   O God help us to see what is beautiful. Fill our hearts with love and kindness and help us to look always for the needs of others. Help us never to be hurtful or unthinking in what we say or do. Amen.

2   Help us, O Lord, to recognise loveliness and beauty wherever it may be and to see in others a reflection of your beauty and truth. Amen.

3   Give to us eyes that we may truly see,
Flight of a bird, the shapes in a tree,
Curve of a hillside, colours in a stone,
Give to us seeing eyes, O Lord. Amen.

Hymns

All things bright and beautiful (WCV 75)
When the world is dark and dreary (SM 54)

~ ~ ~ ~ ~ ~ ~ ~ ~ ~ ~ ~ ~

U is for Unassuming

The preaching of St Francis

To be unassuming is to be modest, quiet and humble. An unassuming person is somebody who gets on quietly with his work without wanting to be noticed or shouting about his own importance. Many unassuming people have become famous. They haven't become well-known because they have drawn attention to themselves, they have become famous because their good lives have stood out as an example.

St Francis is best remembered for his love of wild creatures. He was a very rich young man, with many friends, but he chose to give up his life of luxury and to serve God in a simple way. He chose to have no possessions and to live his life wholly in obedience to God's will. St Francis is remembered for his gentleness, his kindness, and his concern for others.

179

One day a young man asked Francis if he could spend the day with him. He had heard that Francis was an excellent preacher and wanted to copy his ways. Francis agreed to the young man going with him on his day's work, and they set off together. When Francis reached the town he stopped to talk to the children and watch them at play. He went round the market, talking to the stall-holders, sharing their worries, and giving advice and help. When there was heavy work to be done, Francis helped. All day he was kept busy as he moved from one group of people to another. The young man with Francis watched and waited anxiously. The hours were passing and when it came to the afternoon, Francis had still not called the people together to preach to them. Eventually Francis set off again in the direction of home and the young man felt most disappointed. He had spent all day with Francis and his time had been wasted. He had expected to hear a great sermon and Francis had failed to preach at all.

When he asked Francis why he had not preached, Francis was full of surprise. "But I have been preaching all day," he said. "Whenever I visit the sick, or play with the children, or talk with those in the market and share their work, whenever I can bring love, or understanding or comfort to those who need it, then I am preaching God's word. For me there is no other way." Perhaps the young man realised then that the unassuming manner chosen by St Francis was based on the life of Jesus, and no better way exists.

Prayers

1   Dear Lord Jesus, help us to be like you. May we always do our best and may what we do be pleasing to you. Keep us from all conceit and make us glad to serve you in the help we can give to others. Amen.

2   Loving Jesus, gentle lamb,
In your gracious hands I am;
Make me, Saviour, what thou art,
Live yourself within my heart. Amen.

3   Holy God who madest me
And all things else to worship Thee,

Keep me fit in mind and heart
Body and soul to take my part.
Fit to stand and fit to run,
Fit for sorrow, fit for fun,
Fit to work and fit to play,
Fit to face life day by day.
Holy, God, who madest me,
Make me fit to worship Thee. Amen.

4   I come in the little things,
Says the Lord:
Not borne on the morning's wings
Of majesty, but I have set my feet
Amidst the delicate and bladed wheat.

I come in the little things,
Says the Lord:
Yes! on the glancing wing
Of eager birds, and softly pattering feet
Of furred and gentle beasts.

I come in the little things,
Says the Lord. Amen.

Hymns

Morning has broken (WCV 3)
O God thou art the father (WCV 122)

~ ~ ~ ~ ~ ~ ~ ~ ~ ~ ~ ~

U is for Understanding

St Augustine

There was once a great saint called Augustine. He tried to
write a book to explain what God, the Creator, must be
like. He found this extremely difficult, for nobody can
fully understand the love of God.

One day when Augustine was walking by the seashore,
trying to get his thoughts in order, he saw a little boy
playing on the beach. The little boy kept taking his bucket
down to the edge of the sea, filling it with water and
emptying it into a hole he had dug on the beach. St
Augustine watched him for a long time and then asked the
child what he was doing. The little boy said he wanted to
empty all the sea into his hole. St Augustine smiled at the

child, for he knew it was impossible. He lifted the little boy onto his shoulders, so that he could see the great ocean, and he tried to explain to him that he could never succeed. Then St Augustine left the little boy on the beach and continued his walk. He thought about the child and how he had tried to explain to him about the vastness of the sea and then he realised that the task he had set himself was just as impossible as the one the little boy had been trying to do.

To explain who God could be, with all his love and power and might, is impossible. Nobody can understand God. But God himself has already solved the problem. God sent Jesus Christ into the world, to show people the way. If we want to understand God we have to look to the life of Jesus who said, "Anyone who has seen me has seen the Father."

Prayers

1   Day by day, dear Lord of you,
Three things I pray,
To see you more clearly
Love you more dearly
And follow you more nearly
Day by day. Amen.

2   O God, whom only the pure in heart can see,
Grant us to seek for you, and seeking, to find you,
As we find you, so help us to grow in knowledge and
    understanding of you,
Through Jesus Christ our Lord. Amen.

3   God be in my head and in my understanding,
God be in my eyes and in my looking,
God be in my mouth and in my speaking,
God be in my heart and in my thinking,
God be at my end and at my departing. Amen.

Hymns

Wise men seeking Jesus (WCV 58)
The wise may bring their learning (CP 64)

~ ~ ~ ~ ~ ~ ~ ~ ~ ~ ~ ~

U is for Unity
The story of breaking the sticks

When we all gather together for assembly, it give us a feeling of unity. We realise that we belong not only to our class, but also to our school. Each person in the school is important and each one has a special part to play. When someone does something well we all feel proud and happy. But if a member of the school does something unworthy, then we all feel the effect of that, too. That is why everyone in school is equally important from the oldest to the youngest. We all need each other. When we stand together we are strong. If we quarrel and fight among ourselves, we lose our strength. It is a good thing to be united. That way we can achieve great things.

One day a father who had three sons tried to explain to them that they should always stand by each other, to give each other extra support and strength and courage. "If you act together," their father told them, "nobody will be able to break you apart." The father then asked each of his sons to bring him two strong sticks. From each son he took one stick and he bound the three tightly together. When each son presented his second stick, the father took each one and broke it over his knee. The sons watched him in surprise, and when their father had broken the three sticks he then took the bunch of three that he had bound together. The father put all his strength into trying to snap the sticks, but the three tied together proved too strong. "There you are," he told his sons. "Always act together, be united with each other, and no one can destroy you. If you let yourselves become divided, each one of you becomes vulnerable and anyone could break you as I have broken each of your single sticks." The sons understood their father's message. There is strength in unity.

Prayers

1   O God, the Father of all mankind, we bring before you in our prayers today, all your children throughout the world. We praise you for the people of all the different nations. Teach us, by your mercy, how we your children can learn to live in unity, according to your will. Amen.

2   Help us, Almighty Father, to see the world as you
    would have it be. Give us that wonderful gift of love so
    that we may realise that all the world is our neighbour,
    and we are all one in the unity of your great family.
    Amen.

3   Your mercy will not fail us,
    Nor leave your work undone;
    With your right hand to help us,
    The victory shall be won;
    And then, by men and angels,
    Your name shall be adored,
    And this shall be their anthem,
    "One church, one faith, one Lord". Amen.

Hymns

One man's hands can't break a prison down (SM 21)
In Christ there is no East and West (CP 66)

~ ~ ~ ~ ~ ~ ~ ~ ~ ~ ~ ~ ~

V is for Valentine
The blind girl is healed

St Valentine's Day is on 14 February. I expect at this time you have seen the shops filled with cards for people to send to one another as an expression of their love. At this time of the year, too, the days are just beginning to seem a little bit brighter and sunnier after the short dark days of winter. The birds begin to sing again with joy for they feel the first signs of spring in the air. It is said that on St Valentine's Day the birds begin to mate. They start to build their nests and get ready to lay their eggs and hatch their young ones. It is a time of the year when new hope fills the hearts of people and wild creatures alike.

Not a great deal is known about St Valentine. He lived in Rome at a time when it was dangerous to be a Christian. Valentine was determined that as many people as possible should come to know of God's love. In spite of the danger he never ceased to bear witness to his faith. Valentine was taken as a prisoner and he was brought before the Roman emperor for trial. One of the judges was a man called Asternis. One day Asternis was summoned to the court. He came before the emperor and bowed. The emperor said, "Before me stands this prisoner, Valentine. You are to take him to your house, Asternis, and hold him there as a prisoner. He is a Christian and he refuses to give up speaking of Jesus Christ to the people."

Asternis left the court and took with him the prisoner, Valentine, who was bound in chains. When they approached the Asternis' house, Valentine, called out in a fearless voice, "May the Lord bless everyone in this house and help them to know Jesus Christ, who is the light of the world." Asternis stopped suddenly as he listened to these words. "Why do you say Jesus Christ, the light of the world?", he asked Valentine. "Because", replied Valentine, "it is Jesus Christ who can bring light and happiness to everyone."

Waiting for Asternis by the door of his house stood his little daughter. She had been blind since birth and this caused great sorrow to her parents who loved her dearly. They had never heard of Jesus, his love or his teaching. The little girl's life was one of total darkness, without hope.

Asternis spoke to Valentine. "I will put this faith of yours to the test," he said. "You say Jesus Christ is the light of the world and that he brings light and happiness to everyone. Before you stands my little daughter. She has no sight. If you can bring light to her world and restore her sight, then I, too, will become a faithful disciple of Jesus."

Asternis called his daughter and the child came towards him, haltingly, holding out her hands and feeling her way, following the direction of her father's voice. As she came near to them, Valentine reached out his hands and guided the child, so that she stood in front of him. "Lord Jesus Christ," spoke Valentine, "you are the light of the world. Give light to this child of yours, I pray you." And as she stood in front of Valentine, the little girl opened her eyes, and for the first time in her life she could see. The whole household was filled with joy. From that moment not only Asternis, but everyone in the house became Christians. They went with Valentine and they followed in the ways of their new master, Jesus Christ, until the end of their lives.

Prayers

1   Almighty God, giver of life and giver of love, we give you thanks for the re-awakening of the earth, when spring comes round again. We praise you for the bulbs breaking through the soil, the song of birds and the lambs in the field. May we not take these blessings of yours for granted. Amen.

2   O Lord our heavenly Father, from whom comes every good and perfect gift, we thank you for the precious gift of sight. Teach us to see the beauty of the world around us, and may we not have unseeing eyes for the wonders of your kingdom. Amen.

3   Gracious Father, grant your blessing
To your children waiting still.
May we all, your strength possessing,
Learn to do your holy will. Amen.

Hymns

To God who makes all lovely things (WCV 82)
From the darkness came light (CP 29)

~ ~ ~ ~ ~ ~ ~ ~ ~ ~ ~ ~

V is for Valour
Douglas Bader, the pilot

To be valiant is to be brave, especially in battle. There are men and women alive today who have been valiant in times of war and many of them are disabled as a result. The most valiant among them have bravely tried to overcome their difficulties and have gone on living full and useful lives.

One of these famous people was a man called Douglas Bader. He was a pilot before the second world war and when his plane crashed he was very badly injured. Some people in the hospital thought he would die, but Douglas Bader fought for his life and survived. However, both his legs had to be amputated and his future was bleak. Douglas Bader was determined that he was going to learn to fly an aeroplane again. He learnt to walk on his two artificial legs without even using a stick, and eventually could pilot an aeroplane again. When Bader flew during the war he was shot down and became a prisoner of war. In spite of his disabilities, he managed to escape. He proved himself not only a man of true valour, but also one who cared for others. He visited many young people who had lost their legs in terrible accidents. It must have been wonderful for them to see a man like Douglas Bader walking in to visit them in hospital. They must have felt that if he could learn to walk again, then surely they could try to do the same.

Christian soldiers

Christians often like to think of themselves as soldiers. A Christian soldier goes to war against sin, against all that is bad in the world. A Christian soldier has his armour, too. Just as the soldiers have their special boots, and helmets and guns, the armour of the Christian soldier is faith, truth and justice. Christian soldiers need to be brave and valiant, just as the knights of old were.

Some Christian people today belong to a church called the Salvation Army. The officers are valiant people who go out into the towns and help all those who are in need. You may sometimes hear the band of the Salvation Army playing on the streets and hear members of the Salvation

Army reading from the Bible and teaching the people. They are Christian soldiers. The Church of England has a special group of people who work in "The Church Army". They do similar work to that done by the Salvation Army. No matter which church we belong to, we are all members of God's family and each of us is a soldier in the army of Christ. Let us try to be full of faith and full of valour, just like the knights in olden days.

Prayers

1   Give us, O Lord, the strength to do that which is right and always to be valiant, faithful and true. May we be strong in the armour of God and may the shield of God defend us. Help us to become good soldiers of Jesus Christ. Amen.

2   Soldiers, who are Christ's below,
Strong in faith resist the foe:
Boundless is the sure reward
Unto those who serve the Lord. Amen.

3   Let faith be my shield and let joy be my steed
Gainst the dragons of anger, the ogres of greed,
And let me set free with the sword of my youth,
From the castles of darkness, the power of truth.
Amen.

4   Like a mighty army, moves the Church of God,
Brothers, we are treading where the saints have trod;
We are not divided, all one body we,
One in hope and doctrine, one in charity.
Onward, Christian soldiers, marching as to war,
With the cross of Jesus, going on before. Amen.

Hymns

He who would valiant be (WCV 40)
When a knight won his spurs (WCV 66)

~ ~ ~ ~ ~ ~ ~ ~ ~ ~ ~ ~ ~

V is for Vanity

The frog and the geese

There was once a frog who lived on an island all by himself. The only creatures he ever saw were two geese,

188

who used to rest on the island for a while when they were migrating. The frog used to look forward to seeing the geese very much, and he chatted to them whenever they arrived. When the geese were ready to fly again, the frog would say, "Oh how I wish I could leave with you. It's terrible being on this island all alone, month after month." The geese felt sorry for the frog, but they did not want to stay on the island and they could think of no other way to help. So once again they flew away and the frog was left by himself. Then the weather turned bad, and one night there was a terrible storm. The next day the frog hopped all round the island to see if there was any damage, and he saw a strong piece of string that had been washed ashore by the tide. The frog dragged the piece of string to a safe place. He had an idea and he could hardly wait to explain his plan to his friends, the geese.

It was a long time before the geese returned to the island, but at last they came again. The frog could hardly wait to say "Hello" before he started to explain his plan. He told each of the geese to hold an end of the string in its beak, and then he would hold the middle of the string in his mouth. They would then be able to carry the frog over the sea until they reached the mainland. The geese and the frog practised a few times and the plan worked perfectly.

At last the geese and the frog prepared to leave the island for ever and the frog was excited. However, he had to stop talking, for he had to hold the string in his mouth.

Over the sea they flew and soon they were flying above new land, fields and hills and valleys. As the geese flew closer to the ground, people looked up from their work to see them passing overhead. Someone called out, "See how those geese are carrying a frog. What a clever idea! I wonder who could have thought up such a brilliant plan?" Now if the frog had kept quiet all would have been well, but he was so vain and full of his own importance that he couldn't resist pointing to himself and shouting back, "The idea was mine. I am the clever one who thought up the plan!" But, of course, you can guess what happened. As soon as the frog opened his mouth he let go of the string, and down he fell onto the hard earth below and that was the end of him.

Let us learn a lesson from the frog and go quietly about our work each day without boasting or being vain.

Prayers

1   O Lord our God we ask you to take from us the sin of vanity. May we take pride only in the things we do for others and may all our good work and everything that is best in us, be offered back to you with thanks and praise. Amen.

2   Almighty God, who gives grace to the humble, let us not through pride or vanity cause you to be sorrowful. Enable us so to trust in you, that we may always receive the help and guidance of the Holy Spirit; we ask this through Jesus Christ our Lord. Amen.

3   He that is down need fear no fall,
    He that is low, no pride,
    He that is humble ever shall
    Have God to be his guide. Amen.

Hymns

The gospel train's a-coming (SM 55)
Heavenly Father may your blessing (WCV 61)

~ ~ ~ ~ ~ ~ ~ ~ ~ ~ ~ ~ ~

V is for Vexation

The money-changers in the temple

To be vexed is to be angry. It is not a word that we use so much these days as we tend to say angry, or cross, or upset, or annoyed and all these words can have very similar meanings.

There are times when it is right to be angry. When an older child bullies a little one, we are justly angry. When we hear of a group of youths attacking and robbing an old person, we are justly angry. Even Jesus was angry at times.

One day Jesus was going to Jerusalem at the time of the Passover. When he went there, he always liked to visit the temple, and so he made his way there. But instead of the peace and quiet that normally surrounded the building, there were crowds of people shouting and pushing. The traders had set up their stalls and were using the Temple

190

as a market place. There were dealers in cattle, sheep and pigeons, and the money-changers were all seated at their tables. Jesus was so angry that he made a whip out of cords and drove out the traders and their animals. He upset the tables of the money-changers and their coins were scattered everywhere. Then Jesus turned on the dealers in pigeons and he said, "Take them out. You must not turn my Father's house into a market." (John 2: 12–18) He knew that by throwing out the traders he would make them angry with him. But this did not make him afraid or stop him from doing what he knew to be right.

Next time we feel angry let's stop to think if we re justly vexed, or if we are just put out because we have not got our own way. If we are justly angry, let us do something to put matters right.

Prayers

1   O Lord God help us to control our tempers used for selfish reasons, but may we ever be ready to feel truly vexed when we see and hear things that are false, untrue or cruel. We ask this for Jesus Christ's sake. Amen.

2   Do no sinful action
Speak no angry word,
We belong to Jesus,
Children of the Lord.

Christ is kind and gentle
Christ is pure and true,
And we, his little children,
Must be holy too. Amen.

3   When we are sad
And nothing's right,
Although we try
With all our might,
God is with us,
God is with us. Amen.

Hymns

Jesus Lord we look to thee (WCV 62)
No use knocking on the window (100 HT 67)

~ ~ ~ ~ ~ ~ ~ ~ ~ ~ ~ ~

W is for Weddings
Jesus changes water into wine

Jesus was once at a wedding in Cana-in-Galilee. Jesus' mother was among the guests and so were many of Jesus' friends. During the reception, Mary came to Jesus and said, "They have no wine left." (John 2: 3)

Nobody likes to run out of food or drink when they have invited a lot of friends to a special gathering. Mary knew how unhappy this would make everyone and she did not want the day to be spoilt. She went to Jesus, knowing that he would be able to do something about it. When she had spoken to Jesus she said to the servants, "Do whatever he tells you." At the side of the room there were six big stone water-jars. Jesus turned to the servants and told them to fill the jars with water. The servants acted quickly and obediently. When they returned the water-jars had been filled right up to the brim. Jesus said to them, "Now pour out some of the water you have drawn and take it to the steward of the feast." The steward tasted the water and discovered it was the very best wine he had ever tasted. The servants who had filled the jars with water realised that it had turned into wine and they were amazed. The steward called to the bridegroom and said to him, "Everyone else serves the best wine first, but you have not done. You have kept the best wine until now." The bridegroom was delighted to know that there was so much excellent wine still in reserve and the wedding party continued happily.

This was the first miracle which Jesus performed. It must have been wonderful for Mary and Jesus' friends to be present when he began his work of healing and helping. St John says at the end of his account of the wedding celebrations, "This deed at Cana-in-Galilee is the first of the signs by which Jesus revealed his glory and led his disciples to believe in him." (John 2: 11)

Prayers

1 Blessed are you, heavenly Father;
   You give joy to bridegroom and bride.
   Blessed are you, Lord Jesus Christ;

You have brought new life to mankind.
Blessed are you, Holy Spirit of God:
You bring people together in love.
Blessed be Father, Son and Holy Spirit:
One God, to be praised for ever. Amen.

2 Almighty God our heavenly Father, who gave mar-
riage to be a source of blessing to mankind, we thank
you for the joys of family life. May we know your
presence and peace in our homes; fill them with your
love and peace, and use them for your glory, through
Jesus Christ our Lord. Amen.

3 Dear Lord Jesus we ask you to send your special
blessing on all those people we know whose wedding
service we have shared. We ask you to make them
happy, that they may love each other and so bring joy
into their homes. Amen.

4 I saw raindrops on the river.
Love is like the rain,
Bit by bit the river grows,
Till all at once it overflows.
Love is like the rain. Amen.

Hymns

Sing life, sing love, sing Jesus (SM 29)
God is love, his the care (WCV 19)

~ ~ ~ ~ ~ ~ ~ ~ ~ ~ ~ ~

W is for Whitsun

St Peter on the day of Pentecost

Whitsun is one of the great festivals of the Christian year.
It is also known as Pentecost. At this time we remember
how Jesus kept his promise to the disciples. He had told
his friends that when he went back to God his Father in
heaven, he would send the Holy Spirit to be with them
always. Jesus told his friends to wait together in Jerusalem
until he sent his Holy Spirit to them.

On the day of Pentecost, all the disciples were together,
when suddenly the room was filled with a sound like
strong wind. Over the heads of each of the disciples a little

flame of fire seemed to burn. Each of the disciples felt filled with a new life, with a new kind of love and power. They were filled with the Holy Spirit and with this gift they received the ability to speak in different languages, so that everyone would be able to understand them. They found, too, that their minds were full of all the important things they had to say.

Gathered in Jerusalem at that time were people from many different countries who all spoke different languages. But when the disciples stood up to speak, everyone was amazed because each could understand what was being said. Some of them could not believe what was happening and they said rather mockingly. "What can this mean? They have been drinking."

But Peter was now quite fearless of any enemies who may have gathered among the people. He stood before them all and he said firmly, "These men are not drunk as you imagine, for it is only nine in the morning." He went on to address them all saying, "Men of Israel listen to me. I speak of Jesus of Nazareth, a man chosen by God." Peter went on to tell the great crowd to believe in Jesus and follow in his ways. Many of those who listened to Peter on that first Whitsunday were baptised and became Christians. About three thousand people joined the church that day.

Prayers

1 Defend, O Lord, your servants with your heavenly grace, that they may continue yours for ever, and daily increase in your Holy Spirit more and more, until they come to your everlasting kingdom. Amen.

2 Almighty God, who on the day of Pentecost sent your Holy Spirit to the disciples with the wind from heaven and in tongues of flame, filling them with joy and boldness to preach the gospel; send us out in the power of the same Spirit to witness to your truth and to draw all men to the fire of your love; through Jesus Christ our Lord. Amen.

3 Our Father in Heaven, grant that the Holy Spirit may dwell within us; may his power make us strong, may his love make us gentle, may his truth make us free. Amen.

4 O Holy Spirit, help us to be like Jesus and help all Christian people to be like him. Speak to us when we are tempted to do wrong, strengthen us to do right, and show us what we should do. Amen.

5 May the grace of our Lord Jesus Christ, the love of God, and the fellowship of the Holy Spirit be with us all, evermore. Amen.

Hymns

Holy Spirit hear us (WCV 29)
Spirit of God in the clear running water (SM 52)

~ ~ ~ ~ ~ ~ ~ ~ ~ ~ ~ ~ ~

W is for Wilderness

The temptation of Jesus

After Jesus had been baptised by John he wanted to be alone in a quiet place, so that he could talk with God and prepare himself for his work of healing and teaching. Jesus knew that the work ahead of him would be difficult, but he knew that God would guide him and direct him in the right way. But, just as when we try to be good we often fail because we give way to temptation, Jesus, too, was tempted.

Jesus went into the wilderness for forty days and forty nights, and during that time he did not eat. It was then that Satan came to him and said, "If you are the Son of God, tell these stones to become bread." It would have been possible for Jesus to do that. He did use his power to feed the people when they were hungry, but Jesus never used the power of God to make his own way easier. So Jesus sent the devil away when he tempted him in the wilderness.

But Satan did not give up. A second time he came to Jesus. He took him to Jerusalem and set him at the top of the temple. Then he said to Jesus, "If you are the Son of God throw yourself down. The angels of God will hold you up and you will not be hurt." But Jesus answered

195

Satan firmly, saying, "The Bible says, 'You are not to put the Lord your God to the test.'" ᛁ

The devil did not want Jesus to be victorious over him, so he tried a third time. This time he took Jesus to a very high mountain. Far below they could see the kingsdoms of the world. Satan said to Jesus, "All this power and glory will be yours, if you will worship me." But Jesus turned to the devil and said, "Begone, Satan! The Bible says, 'You shall do homage to the Lord your God and worship him alone.'" (Matthew 4: 10–11) The devil finally gave up, and Jesus left the wilderness to begin his work in Galilee.

Sometimes when things seem to go very wrong for us it is like being in the wilderness. Perhaps we need to stay in the wilderness for a little time while we think carefully about what we should do. However, God our Father never leaves us on our own. We can pray to him and to his son, Jesus Christ, and we know that God will make us strong and brave enough to face the things we find difficult. Each one of us has to try to be like Jesus and say "No" when we are tempted to do wrong. If we are determined enough to do this, eventually it will be easier to do what we know is right.

Prayers

1   Almighty God, whose son Jesus Christ fasted forty days in the wilderness, and was tempted as we are, yet without sin: give us grace to discipline ourselves in obedience to your Spirit; and, as we know our weakness, so may we know your power to save; through Jesus Christ our Lord. Amen.

2   Dear Lord Jesus, help us to keep the promises we make in your name, so that we can share in some small measure the temptations that you suffered in the wilderness. Amen.

196

3   Have we trials and temptations?
    Is there trouble anywhere?
    We should never be discouraged:
    Take it to the Lord in prayer.
    Can we find a friend so faithful,
    Who will all our sorrows share?
    Jesus knows our every weakness:
    Take it to the Lord in prayer. Amen.

Hymns

Feed us now O Son of God (SM 4)
There is singing in the desert (CP 26)

~ ~ ~ ~ ~ ~ ~ ~ ~ ~ ~ ~

X is for Multiplication
Noah's Ark

When we multiply we make things bigger. When a seed is sown it produces a single plant which in its turn produces seeds and these eventually produce a good harvest. From such small beginnings great things can grow.

After the great flood, Noah brought all his animals safely out of the ark. He had kept alive two of every living creature, just as God had told him to. God said to Noah, "Come out of the ark, you and your wife, your sons and their wives. Bring out every living creature that is with you, live things of every kind, bird and beast and every reptile that moves on the ground, and let them swarm over the earth and be fruitful and multiply there." (Genesis 8: 16–18) God blessed Noah and his sons, and said to them, "Be fruitful and increase and fill the earth." Then God set his bow in the sky as a sign of his promise that seedtime and harvest, cold and heat, summer and winter, day and night should never cease. And from generation to generation all living creatures have multiplied over the earth and young have been born as the old have died. God creates new life with every fresh season, the earth awakens each year from its winter's sleep.

When Jesus went back to his Father in heaven, he left in Jerusalem the twelve men he had chosen to carry on his work on earth. It must have seemed a very small number to go out into all the world to make people of all nations his disciples, to baptise men everywhere and to teach them all as Jesus had commanded. And yet the disciples had faith. As soon as they were filled with the Holy Spirit they set out in obedience to Jesus' last instructions to them. And from these beginnings sprang the Church of Jesus here on earth. Many have joined God's family and become Christians since the apostles began their teaching. The number has multiplied and multiplied. The word of God is still being spread throughout the world.

Love

Another wonderful gift of God's that spreads and multiplies is the gift of love. Usually if you share or give away what you have, you end up with a little bit less for yourself. With possessions like your toys or your sweets you can see this happening. But no matter how much love we give and share, more love is born within us. The more people we share our love with, the more love there is to pass on. In one hymn, love has been described as a magic penny, and the words tell us exactly how the gift of love is renewed and multiplied:

> Love is something if you give it away,
> Give it away, give it away,
> Love is something if you give it away,
> You end up having more.

> It's just like a magic penny;
> Hold it tight, you won't have any;
> Lend it, spend it, and you'll have so many,
> They'll roll all over the floor!

> So let's go dancing till the break of day,
> And if there's a piper, we can pay,
> For love is something if you give it away,
> You end up having more.

Prayers

1 Little drops of water,
   Little grains of sand,
   Make the mighty ocean
   And the beauteous land.

   Little deeds of kindness,
   Little words of love,
   Make the earth a kingdom.
   Like the heaven above. Amen.

2 Dear Lord Jesus help all the good things we do in our lives to increase and multiply and so yield a rich harvest. We ask this for your name's sake. Amen.

3 Love is a thing we can give or can take,
   Love can bring life or bring death.
   I can love myself and be on the make,
   Or live for others, till my last breath, like Jesus.

Sing life, sing love, sing Jesus,
Sing out whoever you are.
Sing life, sing love, sing Jesus,
Sing out wherever you are. Amen.

Hymns

All people that on earth do dwell (WCV 10)
God is working his purpose out (WCV 72)

~ ~ ~ ~ ~ ~ ~ ~ ~ ~ ~ ~

X is for Voting

Making a choice

The letter "X" is a symbol for many different things.
People who have not learned to read or write or who
cannot hold a pen are allowed to put a cross, like an "X",
where they would usually write their names. "X" can
mean "wrong". "X" is also the sign for multiplication.

Today we are going to think about the cross that we
make when we vote. For example, sometimes you are
asked to vote a captain for a team. In an election, you write
an "X" beside one of the names on the piece of paper, to
show your choice. One of the most important occasions
when people are asked to vote is a general election. Very
many children have a holiday from school on this day.
This is because your school building is needed as a polling
station. Everyone's vote is secret. All people over eighteen
are allowed to vote. Those who are standing for election
may have called at the houses and introduced themselves
to the voters personally.

Whenever you vote you should always think carefully
before marking your ballot paper. You should decide who
you really think will be best person for the job, and not
just hope that your best friend will win.

The ruler and the pearl

A certain rich ruler once had three sons. He loved them all
equally but he wanted to choose one to whom he should
give his very special pearl. He wanted it to be given to the
son who had acted in the most selfless way in the past
month. He filled the court room with a large audience and
told the people they were to vote for the son they thought

200

was the most worthy. Each son was allowed to speak for himself.

The first son told the people that he had been given charge of many jewels. Although he could easily have slipped one of the precious stones into his pocket, he had remained strictly honest, in spite of all temptation.

The people applauded loudly. The first son had done well. Each member of the audience was sure he would receive his vote. The second son then stepped forward.

He told of how, on his travels, he had passed near a river. As he came to the river bank, a child fell into the water. The child was unable to swim and would have drowned if the second son had not, without thought for himself, plunged into the river and rescued the child. The parents were full of gratitude and had offered a rich reward. This he had refused.

The audience listened and were very impressed by the second son's story. They applauded loud and long. Then they waited to hear what the third son would tell.

The third son described how he had come over the mountain and discovered a man who had fallen asleep near the edge of a steep drop. The man, if he moved in his sleep, would surely have rolled over the edge and killed himself. The third son stopped. He intended to waken the sleeping traveller. He then realised he knew the man. He was an old enemy who had often been unkind to him. The third son hesitated. If he were to waken the man, he would arouse the anger of his enemy yet again. The man would accuse him of disturbing his sleep and being a nuisance. However, if the third son left the traveller to his own devices he might fall over the cliff. There was no doubt in the third son's mind. He must wake his enemy and bear the consequences. When he woke the traveller, he turned on the third son and gave him two black eyes.

The audience in the court listened in silence and then they rose to their feet to applaud the worthy action of the third son. The time had come to cast their votes. Who won the ballot and why he was considered the most worthy?

Prayers

1 O God we pray for all who have been elected to form the government of our country. We pray that all who vote, for whatever cause, may ask for your guidance and blessing upon all that shall be done. Amen.

2 Today, O God, we remember those who worked hard to get votes for everyone. Help us as we grow to learn all we can so that we can become responsible citizens of our country. Amen.

3 God be in my head, and in my understanding,
God be in my eyes, and in my looking,
God be in my mouth and in my speaking,
God be in my heart and in my thinking,
God be at my end, and at my departing. Amen.

Hymns

Heavenly Father may your blessing (WCV 61)
Join with me to sing God's praises (CP 30)

~ ~ ~ ~ ~ ~ ~ ~ ~ ~ ~ ~

X is for Xian Aid

The widow's offering

Christian Aid week falls in May. It is a special week in the year when Christians in this country, which is very well off, think especially about the poor in other parts of the world. One of the sayings that Christian Aid uses is that we should "Live more simply that others may simply live." That saying needs very careful thought and it makes us aware that there is very much we could manage without in order that others may have the chance of a better life.

Jesus taught people that they should care for others. He knew that some people were much better off than others and so what each person could give away would be different. After all, if you have 10p and you give away 1p, you have given the same share of what you own as a person who has £100 and can afford to give £10 away. The important thing is for everyone to realise the needs of others, and to give as much as he or she is able.

One day Jesus was standing near the place where

people could give money to the temple funds. He watched many people come past and put quite large sums of money into the chest. They were giving very generously and were probably feeling proud and pleased with themselves for their kindly action. Presently a poor widow came along. When she came close to the treasury chest, she stopped to see what money she had. She took out two very small coins, probably worth about a penny, and quietly and discreetly put them into the chest and continued on her way. Jesus, though, had noticed her and he called the disciples to him. He told them that he had seen the rich people giving large sums and then the small gift of the poor widow. Then Jesus said, "I tell you this. This poor widow has given more than any of the others, for these others who have given had more than enough, but she, with less than enough, has given all that she had to live on." (Mark 12: 43–44)

Whenever we are asked to give to a good cause, whether it is Christian Aid or any other charity, let us try to remember that poor widow. She wanted to do something to help although she had very, very little herself.

Prayers

1   O God, who loves a cheerful giver, help us to find happiness in the things we can do for each other. May we always remember to give a helping hand to those in need and teach us that the joy of giving is the real joy of living. Through Jesus Christ, who gave himself for us. Amen.

2   Help us, Lord Jesus, to be generous; to give away sometimes the things we like, the larger share, the better part. Help us to give up some of our pleasures, if by so doing we give to others a greater good. Let us not think only of ourselves. Let us care for all who are near and dear to you. Amen.

3   Think, think on these things:
Unhappy and lost,
Friendless or old,
Or what it is like
To be hungry, to be cold;
Think, think on these things. Amen.

4   If I should be greedy, get more than my share,
     Just whisper, dear Jesus, there are other folks there
     Who need looking after and just as much care
     As I, who am greedy and not very fair. Amen.

Hymns

I perched in the branches and heard what he said (SM 25)
When God made the garden of creation (CP 16)

~ ~ ~ ~ ~ ~ ~ ~ ~ ~ ~ ~ ~

Y is for Yearning

Simeon sees baby Jesus at the temple

To yearn for something is to long for it, to want it with all your heart. In the Old Testament we can read about men and women who yearned to be close to God. The prophets foretold the coming of the Messiah, the Son of God. They did not know when this great and wonderful event would take place, but they tried to prepare the people to be ready for the Messiah, and they yearned for his coming.

One of the sad things that happened when God sent Jesus Christ to this world was that many people did not recognise who he was. Those who had longed for years and years for the Messiah to come, refused to recognise Jesus when he lived amongst them. Many people continued to yearn for God to fulfil his promise and would not accept Jesus. The prophets had warned that this would happen and events proved them to be right.

However, there were others who had longed to see God and who had waited patiently for his coming. One such person was Simeon. He spent much time in prayer and listened for the voice of God and was always ready to obey. God had promised Simeon that he would not die before he had seen with his own eyes the promised Messiah. Simeon believed with his whole heart that one day he would see God's son and he yearned for that day to come. One day, God told Simeon to go to the temple at Jerusalem. That day Mary and Joseph came to the temple, bringing with them their baby son. They had brought Jesus to the temple to thank God and to offer his life to God's service.

When they entered the temple, Simeon at once recognised the Christ child. His heart filled with joy because his years of yearning were over. He took the baby Jesus from Mary and held him in his arms. What a wonderful moment that must have been for Simeon as he gazed in wonder at the baby and praised God, saying, "Lord, now let your servant go in peace. Your word has been fulfilled. My own eyes have seen the salvation which you have prepared in the sight of every people; a light to reveal you to the nations and the glory of your people Israel."

After that wonderful experience, Simeon's greatest yearning was fulfilled. He told God that whenever death came to him he would be ready because he was at peace. Joseph and Mary too, were full of wonder at all that Simeon had said. They knew he had recognised the baby Jesus as God's own son. Then Simeon blessed them all and spoke to Mary. He told her that she would have to bear much sadness because there were people who would not accept her son and many who would reject him.

Prayers

1 Help us, O Lord, to yearn for you, to watch for you and to wait for you, so that we may always be ready to accept your Holy Spirit into our hearts to direct us in all that we do. Amen.

2 O Heavenly Father, we pray you to send into our hearts and into the hearts of all people everywhere, the spirit of our Lord, Jesus Christ. Amen.

3 Lord we thank you for the pleasure
That our happy lifetime gives;
The inestimable treasure
Of a soul that ever lives;
Minds that look before and after,
Yearning for its home above;
Human tears and human laughter,
And the depth of human love.

For the thrill, the leap, the gladness
Of our pulses flowing free;
Even for each touch of sadness
That may bring us nearer thee;
But above all other kindness,
Thine unutterable love,
Which to heal our sin and blindness
Sent your dear son from above.

Teach us so our days to number,
That we may be early wise;
Dreamy mist or cloud of slumber,
Never dull our heavenward eyes;
Hearty be our work and willing;
As for you, and not for men;
For we know our soul's fulfilling,
Is in heaven, not till then. Amen.

Hymns
Fill thou my life O Lord my God (WCV 11)
For the beauty of this earth (CP 11)

~ ~ ~ ~ ~ ~ ~ ~ ~ ~ ~ ~ ~

Y is for Yoke

The work of the oxen

I am going to read to you some very well known words of
Jesus and then we will think about what they mean. Jesus
said, "Come to me, all whose work is hard, whose load is
heavy; and I will give you relief. Bend your necks to my
yoke, and learn from me, for I am gentle and humble-
hearted; and your souls will find relief. For my yoke is
good to bear, my load is light." (Matthew 11: 28–30)

Jesus liked to watch people at work and he used their
lives to help his followers to learn of God's love. The
farmers had to scatter their seed by hand, and so they
carried a basket of seed round their waist, and walked up
and down the ploughed furrows, scattering the seed as
they went. There were no mechanical ploughs to dig the
earth and prepare the fields for the seeds. Every farmer
kept some oxen, which were yoked together and driven
up and down the fields drawing the ploughs. The oxen
were strong and although the work was slow the animals
were reliable and the farmers knew how to handle them.

The oxen were joined together by carefully shaped
wooden yokes. If a yoke did not fit well it would quickly
make a sore place on the animal's neck. An ox with a
heavy weight to pull and an uncomfortable yoke would be
in great pain, so the farmers had to check the yokes
regularly.

"Come to me"

Jesus grew up in the carpenter's shop in Nazareth. He had
watched Joseph at work and seen the skill he needed to
make a yoke that would be comfortable for the ox. Jesus
learnt the art of carpentry from Joseph. He probably made
many yokes for oxen and he knew how important a
carefully made yoke was. He would not have wanted any
animal to suffer because of a badly-made, ill-fitting yoke.

He would have done the best work he could possibly manage.

And so Jesus turned to the people and said, "Come to me." He promised all those who found their life difficult and their work hard that he would help them and bring them comfort. Jesus would not give to anyone a burden that was too great for them. He would make their load seem easier. He would make sure that the yoke was comfortable. He would lessen people's sorrows and bring them comfort. Jesus would lift the heavy weight of worry from the shoulders of his followers and give them rest. And so many people who have followed his call to come to him have found his words to be true. Hs faithful disciples who have believed and trusted in Jesus have found new life and joy and happiness.

Prayers

1   O Lord Jesus, you said to your friends, "Come unto me." We come to you today and we ask you to help us to carry our burdens and to give us rest when we are tired. Your yoke is easy and your load is light. Help us so to trust in you. Amen.

2   O God, help us to know you that we may truly love you, and so to love you that we may fully serve you, for to serve you is perfect freedom. We ask this through Jesus Christ our Lord. Amen.

3   Give us, O Lord, a steadfast will,
    To meet whatever there may be,
    To face the future unafraid,
    With courage and serenity.
    Give us, O Lord, a heart at peace,
    Our strength sustain, our faith increase. Amen.

Hymns

Come and praise the Lord our King (CP 21)
One more step along the world I go (CP 47)

~ ~ ~ ~ ~ ~ ~ ~ ~ ~ ~ ~ ~

Z is for Zacchaeus

Zacchaeus meets Jesus

Among the people who lived in the city of Jericho was a man called Zacchaeus. He was not at all popular with the people, because he was a tax collector. He was also dishonest and this was much worse. He was a very rich man and he made his wealth by cheating people. He took far too much money from them in taxes and he kept much of it for himself. Because he was so greedy and dishonest, Zacchaeus did not have any friends.

When Zacchaeus heard that Jesus was coming to Jericho he was curious to see him. The fame of Jesus had spread from town to town, and Zacchaeus wondered what exactly Jesus would look like. (Luke 19: 3) When Zacchaeus left his house and came out into the streets he found the whole place crowded with people hoping to catch a glimpse of Jesus. Zacchaeus was a very short man. He could not see over the heads of the people in front of him, and because nobody liked him they would not let him through to the front of the crowd. But Zacchaeus ran on a little way ahead and climbed up into a sycamore tree. He was then high above the crowd and he had an excellent view of the road along which Jesus would soon be passing. He felt very pleased with himself as he peered down from the branches of the tree.

Very soon Jesus came along. He stopped beneath the sycamore tree and he gazed up. "Zacchaeus," he said, "be quick and come down. I want to stay at your house today." (Luke 19: 5) Zacchaeus was stunned. Jesus had stopped and spoken to him. Of all the people in Jericho, he had chosen to stay at the house of the friendless, deceitful tax collector. Zacchaeus climbed down as fast as he could and gladly made Jesus welcome. However, there was disapproval among the people. Why should Jesus choose to spend his time with a man like Zacchaeus? "He has gone to be the guest of a sinner," they said. But Jesus' visit changed the life of the unhappy tax collector. Zacchaeus felt the love and concern Jesus had for him and he became one of Jesus' followers. The whole character of Zacchaeus changed in an instant. He suddenly repented for his past bad ways. "Sir," he said to Jesus, "here and now, I give half my possessions to charity, and if I have cheated anyone, I am ready to repay him four times over." Jesus knew that Zacchaeus meant every word he had said and he replied, "Salvation has come to this house today!" Zacchaeus was as good as his word. He gave away all the goods he had gained through his wrongful acts, and he began to treat the people fairly.

Prayers

1   Dear Lord Jesus, when you visited the home of lonely Zacchaeus, you showed us how you came to be a friend to everyone. Help us, too, to make friends with those who are sad and unhappy. Amen.

2   Think, think on these things:
Forgiving an ill,
Lending a hand,
Or trying to make
Other people understand.
Think, think of these things. Amen.

3   If we look both long and deeply
Into one another's hearts,
We can find the understanding
Tolerance imparts.
Teach us how to look, Lord,
Let us not be blind
To the strength of others
There for us to find. Amen.

Hymns

Think, think on these things (SM 1)
Fisherman, Peter, on the sea (SM 34)

~ ~ ~ ~ ~ ~ ~ ~ ~ ~ ~ ~ ~

Z is for Zeal
William Booth and the Salvation Army

If you are full of zeal, you may have a good cause in which you are very interested and for which you will be prepared to give a great deal of your time and your energy.

The disciples of Jesus were full of zeal when the power of the Holy Spirit was at work within them. They were prepared to go out into the world, no matter how great the danger was to themselves, to spread the teachings of Jesus and to baptise people into the Christian Church.

A zealous person is not put off by the difficulties he faces. He is prepared to meet and overcome every obstacle because of his belief in what he is doing. Since the time of the first apostles there have been very many zealous Christians prepared to fight for what they believed to be right. Many have even faced death rather than give way to those who opposed them.

One man who was born just over 150 years ago showed how the life of one zealous person could change the lives of many others. William Booth was born in Nottingham in 1829. He grew up in a very poor area, and when he was old enough, he had a job in a pawn-shop. Here William Booth discovered how hard life was for those who did not have enough money to eat and dress themselves properly. Many of the people spent what little money they had on drink, because this helped them to forget their problems for a little while. William Booth realised that these people could not help themselves, but no one, not even the government, seemed to care.

William Booth became a preacher in the Methodist Church. He came to London to look for work and discovered far worse poverty than he had ever seen in Nottingham. He invited the poor people into his church, but that offended some of the richer people in his congregation. But William Booth was convinced that as a follower of Jesus he had to be a friend to the friendless. He wanted to provide food, warmth, clothing and shelter for all the people who were in need.

Because his church was against him, William Booth started his own mission in London. He had a small band of helpers and among them was his wife, Catherine, who also did a lot of preaching. Because few of the people William Booth wanted to help came to Church, he went into the streets to them. He and his little band of followers would preach on the street corners, outside public houses or wherever they felt people would listen to them.

They were not always welcomed. William Booth was spat on and had stones hurled at him. But he had such zeal that he carried on with his work. He was a great preacher and often spoke about the war he and his helpers were fighting against poverty and sin. They were soldiers in God's army, fighting the enemy. Booth preached of the salvation of Jesus, of his love for all men shown through his death on the cross. So William Booth's followers became known as the Salvation Army. William Booth himself was the general and others were majors and corporals. The people who came forward to join them increased the size of the Army day by day.

There were still many people who did not like what William Booth was doing. Some thought it was wrong for services to be conducted out of doors to the music of brass bands. Many felt the cheerful hymns were out of place and that their worship was too unconventional. But respect for the work of William Booth and his army was also growing all the time. William Booth never stopped thinking about the people he wanted to serve. He found more and more ways to help the poor. He opened homes for those who had nowhere to go. He started soup-kitchens for those who had nothing to eat. He preached to all men the gospel of love and service, in the way he felt Jesus himself would have chosen. Even people who had been certain that William Booth's missions would fail began to support his work. The Salvation Army spread from London throughout the British Isles, and officers from the army began to travel overseas to take their message to other countries.

When William Booth was buried, many people came to his funeral. The kindness and the goodness of this officer in God's army was known and respected by rich and poor alike. Among the people who mourned his passing was Queen Mary herself. The queen asked a poor woman close to her why she had come to the service and the woman replied, "Well, he cared for the likes of us." The zeal with which William Booth established the Salvation Army has made its work a model for many people today. The army still goes about providing help where it is most needed. The officers always attend to the needs of the poor.

Prayers

1   O God we ask for your blessing on the work of the Salvation Army and all Christian churches that bring comfort and help to those in distress. May they find

joy in service, knowing that whatever they do for others is done for you; and grant that your love may be seen in all that is done in your name; through Jesus Christ our Lord. Amen.

2 O God, give us wisdom to know what is right and make us zealous to do and to declare it. We ask this for your name's sake. Amen.

3 There are hundreds of children,
   Thousand, millions,
   And yet their names are written
   On God's memory,
   There are hundreds and thousands,
   Millions of children,
   But God knows everyone,
   And God knows me. Amen.

Hymns

Onward Christian soldiers (WCV 50)
When I needed a neighbour (CP 65)

~ ~ ~ ~ ~ ~ ~ ~ ~ ~ ~ ~ ~

Theme index

The bold numbers indicate an assembly

People

The bold numbers indicate an assembly

St Andrew **8**
St Augustine 181
Aylward, Gladys 130

Babushka 38
Bader, Douglas 187
Barnado, Dr 67
Bartimaeus **12**
Blondin 173
Booth, William 210
Bruce, Robert 141
Buddha 35

Canute, King 93
St Christopher 128

Damien, Father 99
Daniel **24**
St David **30**
David the Shepherd **27**
Dionysius 105

Elijah **34**

St Francis 179
Fry, Elizabeth **1**

Gandhi **49**
St George **54**
Gideon 145
Goliath **57**

Handel, George 113
Herod, King 38

Isaac **76**

Jacob **79**
Jairus **81**
St John 7
  at the empty tomb 32
  with Jesus and Jairus **81**
John the Baptist 11
Jonah **83**
Joseph **86**

Keller, Helen 46
Kennedy, John F. **90**

Livingstone, David 106
St Luke **103**

Mary Magdalene 32
Moses 22
Muhammad 5

Nightingale, Florence 124
Noah **198**

Offero **128**

St Patrick **136**
St Paul
  his conversion **138**
  his journey with Barnabas **138**
  the shipwreck 173
St Peter
  his denial **143**
  on the feast of Pentecost 193
  the last supper 7
  the rock 155
Prometheus 93

Ruth 15

Samson **160**
Saul, *see* St Paul
Schweitzer, Dr Albert 162
Sheba, Queen of **146**
Siddhartha **35**
Simeon 205
Solomon 146
St Stephen 158
Sullivan, Anne 46

St Thomas 154

St Valentine **185**

William Tell 26
Wilkinson, Kitty 60

Zacchaeus **209**

Events and festivals

The bold numbers indicate an assembly

Parables, legends and stories

The bold numbers indicate an assembly

Biblical index

Old Testament

The bold numbers indicate an assembly

New Testament